History of Christianity

*Discovering Lost Stories from the
Christian World*

Free Bonus from Captivating History (Available for a Limited time)

Hi History Lovers!

Now you have a chance to join our exclusive history list so you can get your first history ebook for free as well as discounts and a potential to get more history books for free!

Simply visit the link below to join.

Or, Scan the QR code!

captivatinghistory.com/ebook

Also, make sure to follow us on Facebook, X, and YouTube by searching for Captivating History.

Table of Contents

INTRODUCTION 1

CHAPTER 1 - FORGOTTEN ORIGINS: EARLY CHRISTIAN COMMUNITIES BEYOND THE ROMAN EMPIRE 3

CHAPTER 2 - THE LOST GOSPELS: UNCOVERING THE APOCRYPHAL SCRIPTURES 18

CHAPTER 3 - THE FORGOTTEN APOSTLES: THE QUIET WORKERS OF CHRISTIANITY 25

CHAPTER 4 - THE DESERT FATHERS: MYSTICS AND MONASTICS OF THE EARLY FAITH 38

CHAPTER 5 - WOMEN OF THE CROSS: THE LESSER-KNOWN HOLY WOMEN OF CHRISTIANITY 51

CHAPTER 6 - THE GOSPEL IN THE FAR EAST: CHRISTIANITY'S JOURNEY TO CHINA, KOREA, AND JAPAN 67

CHAPTER 7 - FAITH ON THE FRINGES: CHRISTIANITY IN THE CELTIC LANDS 82

CHAPTER 8 - CHRISTIANITY AND ISLAM: THE SURVIVAL OF CHRISTIAN COMMUNITIES AFTER THE MUSLIM CONQUEST 94

CHAPTER 9 - THE CRUSADERS' BLIND SPOT: BROTHERS IN NAME, STRANGERS IN SPIRIT 106

CONCLUSION 117

HERE'S ANOTHER BOOK BY MATT CLAYTON THAT YOU MIGHT LIKE 119

FREE BONUS FROM CAPTIVATING HISTORY (AVAILABLE FOR A LIMITED TIME) 120

BIBLIOGRAPHY 121

IMAGE SOURCES 124

Introduction

More often than not, the story of Christianity is told in broad, sweeping strokes. Many books begin immediately with a scene in Bethlehem before their next chapters move on to Jerusalem, Rome, Byzantium, and, eventually, the cathedrals in Europe. The main characters are often emperors, their councils, martyrs, and missionaries. These, however, barely scratch the surface of the topic. It is safe to conclude that the history of Christianity is vast and complex—so vast, in fact, that entire volumes have been written just to cover its first few centuries. But although the shelves have already been filled with theological tomes and historical pieces, much of Christian history remains hidden in the margins.

This book was written specifically about those margins.

Instead of filling the pages to retell the grand narrative of the faith from start to finish, each chapter of this book revolves around the lesser-known corners. It covers stories that are left almost forgotten in the deserts, lost gospels, overlooked saints, and the distant lands where Christianity took root in ways many are unfamiliar with today. So many have retold the story of Peter in Rome or even Paul's journey across the Mediterranean. However, what about Thomas, whose reluctance to travel beyond Jerusalem eventually led him to India? Few have heard of a certain warrior queen whose path to vengeance led her to become a saint. What about the Christians who prayed in Aramaic centuries after Latin became the church's preferred language? What about those lands on a completely different continent, like China and Japan? How did Christianity arrive at their royal courts?

Indeed, the history of Christianity is not tied in a single thread. Instead, it is a large tapestry that has been woven from countless voices. Some were loud, clear, and influential, while others were fainter yet still enduring. Typically, the loudest voices—those of emperors, popes, and powerful councils—are the ones more easily and commonly remembered. But beneath those voices, one can find an array of others, each with a different story to tell. There are voices of women who led quietly but faithfully, of communities that lived on the fringes of an empire, and of gospels that were once widely disseminated and later buried deep beneath the sands. These voices shaped Christianity just as much as the creeds and councils, even if history has not always remembered them kindly.

Exploring these lesser-known paths does not mean that we are rewriting the story of Christianity. By doing this, we are broadening the chapters. We are seeing the stories unfurl not only through the massive windows of cathedrals but also through the doors of caves, ships, and side streets. We are stepping away from the spotlight to walk among the ordinary, the local, and the nearly forgotten.

Suffice it to say that this book is specially made for the curious, for those who wish to know what else happened in the regions far beyond Rome and Constantinople. This book is written for those who sense that Christianity's past is deeper, stranger, and, of course, more beautiful than the outlines we often hear. The chapters in this book do not cover the full history of the religion, but it is a journey through the lesser-known stories of the Christian faith that are often overlooked.

Chapter 1 – Forgotten Origins: Early Christian Communities Beyond the Roman Empire

Whenever people mention the history of early Christianity, many cannot help but immediately think of the Roman Empire. Some may picture a scene of the brutal persecutions or even an episode where Christians faced their martyrdom in the Colosseum before cheering Romans. Others may think of Emperor Constantine, whose decree finally legalized the faith, ushering in a whole new era of Christian dominance. Indeed, the history of Christianity is intertwined with Rome and its many emperors. Yet, few are aware that beyond the Eternal City, far from the watchful gaze of the Caesars, the religion was quietly being spread, eventually welcoming new believers.

The Persian Empire, for instance, was a realm dominated by fire, a symbol of the age-old faith of its people. Sacred flames could often be seen burning eternally atop temple altars. The Persians were firm believers of Zoroastrianism. From their point of view, this ancient religion was more than a belief system; it was also the very foundation of their empire's identity. The Persians, including kings, queens, and the highest-ranking officials, held the god Ahura Mazda in the highest reverence. Considered the supreme god of Zoroastrianism, Ahura Mazda was the creator of all beings. The deity was described as wise and good.

Yet, the vast empire was no monolith of faith. The lands were home to a mosaic of different people. Cities like Susa, Babylon, and Ctesiphon were home to many Jews. Hellenistic cults also existed in Persia ever since the time Babylon was conquered by Alexander the Great. Buddhist influences also lingered, particularly during the Sasanian period (224-651 CE). Of course, the Persian authorities were always watchful. Foreign religions were tolerated but only to a point; the faith should not challenge the authority of the Shahanshah, or the King of Kings. Those who crossed the line would undoubtedly face retaliation, usually in the most brutal way a human could ever think of.

Christianity did not arrive in Persia through conquest. Instead, the faith took its first step into the empire through whispers carried by traders, migrants, and even captives. The religion spread along the very same routes that brought silk and spices into the empire. Typically, word of this new faith was discussed among merchants who learned of the religion during their travels to Syria and Mesopotamia. The first Christian communities emerged by the 2nd century CE. It did not start in the heart of the empire but in its western provinces, particularly among the Aramaic-speaking populations of Edessa (modern-day Urfa), Nisibis, and Seleucia-Ctesiphon.

However, these early believers were influenced by Syriac traditions rather than the Romans. They practiced a form of Christianity that appears distinct from that of the Latin and Greek worlds. Of course, the spread of the religion started off slowly and quietly, often attracting the Jewish communities that had long called the Persian cities their home. Unfortunately, as the faith rose in popularity, suspicion began to grow. The Persian kings grew restless, especially since Christianity had ties to Rome (by this time, Constantine had already risen as the emperor, making Christianity the dominant religion of the empire), which was their ultimate rival. The Persian authorities began to see the followers of Christ as potential threats instead of harmless worshipers. They previously tolerated the faith, but that was in the past.

Under Constantine, the Christian Romans could breathe easy. The same, however, could not be said of the Persians. In 339 CE, the reigning Persian king, Shapur II, launched a massive persecution. As a result, sixteen thousand Christians were martyred, including Miles, Bishop of Susa. Despite the hostilities, Christianity never disappeared from Persia. The faith endured through multiple episodes of suppression and resurgence. By the 5th century CE, the Church of the

East (also known as the Nestorian Church) had been firmly established in Persia. Distinguishing itself from Western Christianity, it bloomed in regions far beyond the borders of Persia, making its influence known as far as China.

The martyrdom of Miles, Bishop of Susa.[1]

Similar to both Rome and Persia, Armenia had an ancient belief system that honored a pantheon of gods. Before the introduction of Christianity, the Armenians prayed to gods who reflected the kingdom's rugged landscape—from fierce war gods to divine beings who controlled the weather and fertility deities tied to the unpredictable rhythms of nature. Their chief deity was known as Aramazd, which was a derivative of the Persian Ahura Mazda, who reigned from the heavens with the goddess Anahit and the warrior god Vahagn. However, over time, Armenia would experience a change in faith.

Faith often found itself entangled with politics. The Armenians were well aware of this. They knew that if they were to align too closely with Persia, their kingdom would face merciless aggression by the Romans. If they leaned too much toward Rome, the Persians would not hesitate to show their wrath. Despite being known as proud and independent, the noble houses of Armenia knew they were nothing more than pawns in the eyes of these colossal powers. So, they were careful to keep themselves balanced. They adopted elements from both the Roman and

Persian empires, yet they never fully surrendered to either. However, the arrival of Christianity in the kingdom would soon disrupt this balance. While Armenian pagan and Zoroastrian temples could stand side by side, being influenced by both Persian and Hellenistic traditions, Christianity demanded exclusive devotion.

Meanwhile, beyond the shifting sands of Egypt and across the Red Sea, one could find the Kingdom of Aksum (modern-day Ethiopia), with its obelisks piercing the sky and its busy ports. The kings of Aksum were believed to have traced their lineage back to the union of Solomon and the Queen of Sheba. Similar to its neighboring kingdoms, Aksum was also a land of many faiths, as it was a melting pot of trade and migration. While the gods of South Arabia were once held in high honor there, the kingdom also had Jewish settlements. It is interesting to think that even in a region as far as Africa's highlands, traditions from the Mediterranean and the Near East found a foothold.

Aksum was a land where religious identity was fluid. Aksumite nobles could offer prayers to Arabian deities one day and conduct business with Jewish traders the next day. Even the Aksumite rulers never declared allegiance to a specific faith, allowing different traditions and beliefs to coexist. This was done to ensure that no power, be it local or foreign, could dominate the spiritual sphere. Yet, when a certain missionary came to the kingdom, everything changed.

The Missionaries Who Brought Christianity to These Lands

The spread of Christianity was not always driven by conquest. More often than not, the faith traveled quietly. Instead of being carried by armies, the religion was introduced by individuals whose conviction and devotion were stronger than a battalion of soldiers. These individuals were missionaries, pilgrims, or simply wanderers who embarked on a journey far beyond the comfort of their homeland to share a message.

Among the first to embark on such a journey was Saint Thomas. Hailing all the way from Roman Judea, he was known to have carried the teachings of Christ to a whole different continent. He was believed to have reached India, where Hinduism and Buddhism had been the primary beliefs of the locals for many centuries. In a land rich in spiritual traditions, Thomas's journey was undoubtedly full of obstacles. Although his mission ended in his martyrdom, Thomas was able to spread the gospel. His legacy endures through the Nasrani Christians of India, who blend their Syriac Christian heritage with local traditions.

Of course, Thomas was not the only one who traveled far to share the Lord's message. In other corners of the world, other figures would rise, stopping at nothing to spread the faith. Some came from a noble background, while others were outcasts or slaves who succeeded in rising through the ranks. Their words reshaped kingdoms, and their sacrifices forged the path for Christianity to prevail.

Gregory the Illuminator and Armenia

Gregory's life was fraught with peril even from the beginning. He was the son of a Parthian nobleman named Anak. Ancient records claimed that Anak was sent to Armenia by the Persians. This was a time when Persia and Rome were in conflict. His task was to infiltrate the kingdom under the pretense of friendship. This was because the ruling Armenian king, Khosrov II, was pro-Roman, and the Persians planned to weaken his reign. Long story short, Anak succeeded in luring Khosrov II into a trap and assassinated him. While some were certain that he killed the Armenian king under Persian orders, others claimed Anak had a personal vendetta against him. Regardless of the reason, the murder resulted in the execution of Anak's entire family by Armenian nobles. Only Gregory survived since he was only an infant at the time.

Mosaic art depicting Gregory the Illuminator.[2]

Armenia was not safe for the infant Gregory. He was smuggled into the Byzantine Empire. He lived his early life in Caesarea (modern-day Turkey), where he was educated in Christianity. However, instead of remaining within the safe walls of the city, Gregory soon embarked on a mission to spread the faith. He eventually returned to Armenia; luckily, no one recognized him. Gregory offered himself to become a servant of the ruling king, Tiridates III, the very son of the ruler whom Anak had murdered. Without revealing his lineage, he served in Tiridates's court as either a royal courtier or attendant.

But the truth was meant to come out. During a royal festival, the king, who was a devout follower of Armenian pagan traditions, ordered Gregory to pay his respect to the goddess Anahit. After all, it was common for those in his position to place an offering to the goddess. However, Gregory was a devout Christian; he refused to make the offering and proclaimed that he would only worship the Christian god.

"How dare you disobey me!" King Tiridates might have exclaimed.

Again, Gregory refused to lay his offering down. This further enraged the king, who ordered an investigation of his background. When it was revealed that Gregory was the son of his father's murderer, the king immediately ordered his punishment. Gregory, who was once one of the king's most trusted courtiers, was thrown into the deep underground dungeon of Khor Virap. At this point, it appeared as if there was no hope for Gregory to survive; the dungeon was a notorious prison where inmates were often left to die.

Khor Virap, a monastery built on the very site where Gregory was once imprisoned.³

Perhaps God was looking after him. For thirteen years, Gregory survived. This was because of a kind-hearted woman, who many believed was also a Christian. She secretly lowered scraps of food to him. One day, Tiridates was struck by a mysterious illness. Some sources claimed that the king turned mad and could often be seen roaming the wilderness like a wild beast. Others spoke of his body becoming deformed. Many viewed his condition as a form of punishment for his brutal persecution of Christians; the king was the one responsible for executing Saint Hripsime.

No priest or healer could cure him. The royal court was growing restless until one of the royal family members had a vision. The vision spoke of the only man who could cure the king. This person, however, had been condemned to death. The court realized that it was none other than Gregory, so he was quickly removed from Khor Virap. He was then brought before the king. Despite being left to die, Gregory never planned on exacting revenge. Instead, he prayed over Tiridates, invoking God's power.

Much to the surprise of many, Tiridates was healed. His madness was lifted, and his body regained strength. After witnessing the miracle of the Christian God firsthand, the king repented. He pledged to follow Gregory's faith. Armenia witnessed a change. In 301 CE, Tiridates declared Armenia a Christian kingdom, becoming the very first nation to adopt the faith as its state religion.

The Arrival of Christianity in Iberia

The transformation of the Kingdom of Iberia (in what is now Georgia) into a Christian kingdom is traditionally credited to Saint Nino. Considered a somewhat mysterious yet influential figure, Saint Nino was a female missionary who hailed from Cappadocia. Georgian tradition has it that Saint Nino arrived in Iberia sometime in the early 4th century CE upon experiencing a divine calling. She was said to have carried nothing but a cross made of grapevines bound with her own strands of hair. Her teachings and miraculous healings quickly attracted the attention of the locals. Eventually, Saint Nino succeeded in reaching the royal court of King Mirian III and Queen Nana.

An icon of Saint Nino, displayed at Svetitskhoveli Cathedral.'

Of course, the king was initially met with skepticism. After all, the dominant belief system of the kingdom was paganism, which was heavily influenced by Zoroastrianism. However, the king soon changed his mind after experiencing a dramatic event. Tradition narrated that the episode began when the king was out hunting in the forest. All of a sudden, darkness befell him; the king had been struck blind. He walked without direction. Each minute that passed by, he could feel his panic and desperation grow. The king was lost deep in the forest he knew so well. He prayed to his pagan gods, the very ones he had worshiped for decades, yet he received no answer. So, King Mirian decided to plead to a god whom he had no knowledge of: the God that Saint Nino had preached to him previously. Almost instantly, his vision was restored.

The king could finally breathe easy. Completely overwhelmed by what he perceived as a divine miracle, the king did not hesitate to convert to Christianity in 337 CE. Shortly after—possibly in the same year—King Mirian declared Christianity the state religion of Iberia. With royal support, more churches began to dot the region, and the faith spread rapidly. One of the earliest Christian sites in Georgia, known as the Svetitskhoveli Cathedral, became the heart of the Georgian Orthodox Church. Despite the many external pressures that emerged years later, Christianity survived and remained strong in Georgian culture. Even when the region fell under Mongol, Persian, and Ottoman rule, its unique Christian traditions persisted. Today, the Georgian Orthodox Church remains one of the most ancient Christian institutions, with a faith that has been continuously practiced for over 1,600 years.

Frumentius and the Christian Kingdom of Ethiopia

The story of how the Kingdom of Aksum (modern-day Ethiopia and Eritrea) embraced Christianity began with two brothers, Frumentius and Aedesius. Originally from Tyre (located in modern-day Lebanon), the brothers embarked on a journey across the Red Sea. Things took a dark turn when their ship was suddenly attacked by pirates off the coast of the Kingdom of Aksum. A violent scene ensued. These merciless pirates massacred the entire crew. They spared Frumentius and Aedesius, only to take

An icon of Saint Frumentius.[5]

them as captives. The brothers were then transported to the royal court of Aksum. This was the moment when their freedom became a thing of the past, as the two brothers were given to the Aksumite king.

However, Frumentius and Aedesius did not remain slaves. With their intelligence—they both received an education, an opportunity that was not given to everyone—the brothers gained the king's trust, eventually rising through the ranks. While Aedesius was made the king's cupbearer, Frumentius served as his secretary. They did not lose their positions when the king died. Frumentius, in particular, served as an advisor to the queen regent, who ruled the kingdom on behalf of the young Prince Ezana.

It was during this time that Frumentius began spreading Christian teachings. He encouraged Christian merchants and traders who docked at the kingdom's harbors to practice their faith openly. Christian places of worship were also established in preparation for Aksum's conversion years later.

When Ezana finally reached the ripe age to rule, Frumentius and Aedesius were finally granted their freedom. Aedesius returned to Tyre, but Frumentius had another plan. Instead of returning to his homeland, which he had left decades ago, he went to Alexandria to seek Patriarch Athanasius. He hoped that with the patriarch's help, missionaries would be deployed to Aksum. However, in a turn of events, Athanasius made him the first bishop of Aksum. Frumentius wasted no time in returning to Aksum.

He taught King Ezana about Christianity, which eventually led to the king's baptism. While it could be plausible that his conversion was due to his interest in the faith, another reason behind his decision was his desire to solidify the kingdom's trading relationship with the Roman Empire. The king also hoped that his conversion could unify the diverse peoples of the Kingdom of Aksum. Therefore, to realize this, Ezana declared Christianity the state religion of Aksum, making Ethiopia one of the earliest Christian kingdoms. The king even issued coins with the Christian cross. This marked Aksum's official transition to Christianity.

The Church of Our Lady Mary of Zion.⁶

To further solidify his kingdom's Christian identity, Ezana also commissioned the construction of churches across the region, including the most famous of all, the Church of Our Lady Mary of Zion. Constructed in the 4th century, the church gained even greater significance following an extraordinary claim. Many believed that the church was where the Ark of the Covenant was stored. According to biblical tradition, this sacred chest contained the stone tablets of the Ten Commandments. To this day, Ethiopian Christians hold that the Ark of the Covenant is indeed still in the church, guarded by only a single monk who is allowed to see it.

An illustration of Moses and Joshua bowing before the Ark of the Covenant.[7]

How Christianity Influenced These Nations

While Christianity in Rome and Constantinople was shaped by the Latin (Roman Catholic) and Greek (Eastern Orthodox) traditions, Christian communities beyond these regions, such as Persia, Armenia, and Ethiopia, also had developed their own unique ways of practicing the faith.

The Syriac Peshitta, for instance, played a pivotal role in shaping Eastern Christianity. It was a translation of the Bible into Syriac, a dialect of Aramaic, which was also the language spoken by Jesus Christ himself. In contrast to the Latin Vulgate (used in the West) and the Greek

Septuagint (used by the Byzantines), the Peshitta kept the linguistic and cultural essence of early Christianity intact. This made the gospel more accessible, especially to those in the eastern regions of the Christian world. Since it was written in a language close to what the Lord once spoke in, the Peshitta led to the emergence of a unique theological tradition completely separate from Western Christianity. To put it simply, it preserved early Christian teachings in a way that felt more authentic to the local believers.

Apart from theology, these communities also left a unique mark on Christian art and iconography. The Armenians, in particular, were experts in illuminated manuscripts. These are handwritten religious texts that feature detailed illustrations. Biblical scenes were painted with influences from Armenia's own artistic heritage. Figures on the manuscripts often appeared in vibrant yet delicate colors, making them distinct from those in the Byzantine Empire.

Ethiopia also had its own distinguished art form. Their religious murals could often be seen covering the walls of their rock-hewn churches. Figures were usually painted with bold outlines and expressive eyes. Their robes typically appeared in colors inspired by the earth. The Ethiopians also made sure to portray biblical figures not as foreign icons. Instead, they had features of the land's people, with dark skin and curly hair.

An example of an Ethiopian biblical manuscript.'

Meanwhile, the Persians blended Christian themes with the intricate floral and geometric designs of Zoroastrian and Buddhist traditions. As Nestorian Christians traveled across Central Asia, they also adapted their religious imagery to reflect the cultures they encountered. More often than not, their art featured haloed saints with Central Asian features. The crosses were also decorated with Persian-style motifs, which clearly showed how Christianity had merged with local artistic traditions.

An example of Persian art.[9]

However, despite all of these years on the rise, these Christian communities were not immune to the tides of history. Persia, for one, saw a change in its religious landscape when Islamic influence began to rise tremendously in the 7th century. The once-powerful Zoroastrian empire fell and, with it, the fragile position of Persian Christians. However, since Islamic teachings viewed the Christians (along with Jews and Sabians) as People of the Book, those Persians were not forced to convert to Islam immediately. They were allowed to worship in their churches and were granted protection. In return, the Christians had to pay a special tax called the jizya.

As time passed, Arabic replaced Syriac as the dominant language of administration and worship in some Christian communities. Churches were eventually abandoned since there was an increase in the number of Christians converting to Islam; some did so voluntarily, but there were also those who converted due to social or economic pressures. Peace, however, was not always present. During certain periods, Christians were left with no choice but to endure increasing restrictions. They had to pay higher taxes, face social limitations, and occasionally face the destruction of churches. In the end, Persia saw a permanent change. Many Persian Christians either migrated to Christian territories or converted to Islam. This led to the near disappearance of the once-flourishing Christian communities in the nation.

Almost the same could be said of Armenia. When the Byzantine Empire fell in 1453, Armenia was brought under the influence of the Ottoman Empire. Under the Ottomans, Armenian Christians were considered dhimmis (protected second-class citizens). Similar to the case in Persia, the Ottomans tolerated Christianity, but Christians had to face heavy taxation and restrictions on church construction. Legal discrimination was the norm. The worst episode of suffering came in the 19th and early 20th centuries. Suspected of supporting Russia, massacres were conducted in the 1890s. The later Armenian Genocide lasted from 1915 to 1917. These two years of brutality claimed the lives of over 600,000 Armenian Christians. Nevertheless, unlike Persia, Christianity prevailed in Armenia despite centuries of hardship. To this day, the Armenian Apostolic Church remains the core of Armenian identity. Although its population had been greatly reduced during the genocide, Armenia remains a Christian nation.

Ethiopia fared slightly better compared to Armenia. When Islam was on the rise, making its mark on North Africa and the Middle East, Ethiopia's ties with the wider Christian world (the Byzantine Empire, Egypt, and the Holy Land) were cut off. Since Islamic states controlled the Red Sea trade routes, Ethiopia was geographically and politically isolated from other Christian nations. Regardless of this, the nation's unique religious traditions endured. Ethiopia nearly collapsed when the Muslim leader from the Adal Sultanate, Ahmad ibn Ibrahim al Ghazi, launched his attacks. Luckily, with military support from the Portuguese, Ethiopia survived. Jesuit missionaries once attempted to impose Catholicism on the nation to no avail. Today, Ethiopian Christianity remains strong, with the Ethiopian Orthodox Tewahedo Church preserving its ancient tradition.

The Silk Road also experienced a decline of its Christian communities. Initially, Mongol rulers like Genghis Khan and his immediate successors, like Ögedei and Möngke, offered religious tolerance. This allowed Nestorian Christianity to bloom alongside Buddhism and Islam. Christianity was popular, especially among Turkic and Mongol tribes of Central Asia. The faith even gained influence in the Mongolian court itself. Some Mongolian queens and nobility were Christians, and Nestorian priests influenced both diplomatic and religious affairs.

However, this all changed when the Mongol rulers, like Ghazan Khan, eventually converted to Islam. This ushered in a brief period when Christian influence waned. Not only did Christian communities lose political influence, but many churches that had once flourished in cities of Central Asia, like Merv and Samarkand, became a shadow of their past. Though not forcibly destroyed, many of them were gradually neglected.

Nevertheless, these early Christian communities' legacy was never meant to be completely erased. Traces of their presence continued to live on in ancient scriptures, ruins, arts, and traditions. Their voices can still be heard in the rock-hewn churches of Ethiopia, in the illuminated manuscripts of Armenia, and in the rare surviving Syriac texts of Persia.

Chapter 2 – The Lost Gospels: Uncovering the Apocryphal Scriptures

A great discovery was about to take place in the winter of 1945. It began with a young farmer named Muhammad 'Ali al-Samman in the Egyptian desert near the village of Nag Hammadi. He was out digging for fertilizer near the base of a cliff. As he dug, the farmer suddenly struck a red clay jay that had long been buried beneath the sand. He hesitated to open it at first, as the farmer was a superstitious man. Egypt was, after all, well known for its curses. However, curiosity soon got the best of him. He smashed it open.

Inside was neither gold, relics, nor treasure. Instead, the farmer found thirteen leather-bound papyrus codices (ancient manuscripts), tightly packed with ancient pages. He was familiar with the script since the language used was Coptic. The content, however, would startle the modern world. These texts were gospels and sayings of Jesus that no one had read for centuries—perhaps some had never been seen before. Later known as the Nag Hammadi library, some claim these pages were hidden away intentionally during the early centuries of Christianity.

Among these pages, one could find the Gospel of Thomas, which did not talk about crucifixion or resurrection but rather a stream of mysterious sayings believed to be attributed to Jesus. There was also a gospel that described, in detail, a scene where Jesus ascended and was resurrected, which the Bible never mentions. Others were even more cryptic; there were mystical texts layered with symbols and visions, hinting at a world of Christian belief that had been lost, silenced, or simply left behind.

Believe it or not, these were not counterfeit gospels. They were real expressions of faith from real Christian communities that had been pushed to the margins as orthodoxy took shape.

What Are the Apocryphal Gospels?

Language-wise, the word "apocryphal" comes from the Greek *apokryphos*, meaning "hidden" or "secret." In Christian history, the apocryphal gospels refer to writings about Jesus and his teachings that never made it into the New Testament canon. Some of them were authored by early Christians, who believed they were passing on fundamental teachings of Jesus based on how they understood the Lord. Others were written by those who belonged to certain communities, mostly those with different theological ideas or cultural contexts.

Compared to the four canonical gospels—Matthew, Mark, Luke, and John—these apocryphal gospels offer alternative perspectives on Jesus's life, words, and meaning. While some were only a simple collection of sayings, some recount miracles, private dialogues, and post-resurrection visions.

These texts were excluded from the Bible, but they were not necessarily rejected because they were poorly written or lacked spiritual value. In fact, in the first few centuries after Jesus, many Christian communities read and revered them. Scholars suggest that the Gospel of Thomas, for instance, was likely read by those in Syria or Egypt at the same time as the Gospel of John. While the Gospel of Peter was circulated in parts of Asia Minor, the Gospel of Mary was better known in Christian circles that had a high regard for Mary Magdalene's role in the story of Jesus.

The Apocryphal Gospels of Thomas, Mary, Peter, and Bartholomew

Many may agree that the Gospel of Thomas was unlike anything in the New Testament. There was neither a narrative nor miracles. There was no story of a virgin birth or crucifixion. There was no resurrection. Instead, it opened with a brief introduction, identifying the text as a collection of secret teachings spoken by the living Jesus and recorded by the Apostle Thomas.

This particular gospel was a collection of 114 sayings. Believed to have been recorded by the Apostle Thomas, they were teachings that Jesus was said to have imparted. Although some of the sayings may sound familiar, like lines found in both Matthew and Luke, others were strikingly different. These unfamiliar ones sounded rather mysterious and poetic. Most importantly, they focused on what is hidden within. One teaching, for example, suggests that the divine presence can be found in ordinary, physical things, such as beneath the surface of wood or stone, places that are often overlooked.

Instead of highlighting miracles or sacrifice, the Gospel of Thomas speaks of inner discovery. It paints Jesus as someone who spoke like a sage or mystic, inviting his listeners not to believe in him but to seek the truth within themselves. This gospel claimed that salvation did not come through his death but instead through recognizing a divine spark within oneself. There was no talk about atonement or even blood on a cross. There was an emphasis on how the Kingdom of God is not something to wait for; it is already here, hidden in plain sight.

Scholars suggest that this gospel may date as early as the late 1st century. It is possibly contemporary with the canonical gospels. However, it is also plausible that it was not compiled until the 2nd century. It has also been suggested that the gospel was written in either Syria or Egypt, where early Christian mysticism and Gnostic tendencies were beginning to develop.

The gospel seemed extremely individualistic and too mystical. It differed too much from the message that centered on Jesus's death and resurrection. It clearly did not fit the teachings that the early Christian Church was trying to define. So, the Gospel of Thomas was eventually left out of the canon. However, it was never declared heretical. To this day, this collection of mysterious sayings remains one of the oldest and most intriguing Christian texts. It gave us a window to peek at a time when believers were still trying to understand what kind of teacher and savior Jesus really was.

Another one of the earliest surviving Christian texts was the Gospel of Mary. With one of the central themes being women's leadership and spiritual authority, the text survives only in fragments, with its beginning and middle sections missing. While the two shorter Greek fragments covered only a small portion of the gospel, the 5th-century manuscript now known as the Berlin Codex (discovered in the late 19th century and written in Coptic) is considered the most complete version. Still, the first six pages are missing.

Despite not being complete, the manuscript sheds a different light on Mary Magdalene. The gospel offers a bold and unusual voice in early Christianity. Mary Magdalene is painted not merely as a side character but as a spiritual leader. The story was set after Jesus's departure. The text begins with the disciples in fear and confusion—that was, until Mary spoke. She offered comfort and revealed the teachings the Lord had shared with her in private. They were teachings about the soul, peace, and overcoming fear.

However, not everyone was eager to listen to her. Peter, for one, began questioning Mary's authority.

"Why would Jesus reveal these teachings to a woman?" he questioned.

His doubt was shut down by Levi, who defended Mary. "Who are we to challenge someone that the Savior clearly trusted?"

Like the Gospel of Thomas, this particular gospel was not included in the New Testament canon. This was likely due to its emphasis on inner knowledge, its non-hierarchical view of leadership, and the fact that it gave a crucial role to a woman. Regardless, this gospel tells us that some early Christians held Mary Magdalene in a higher regard; she was not seen as only a witness to Jesus's life but also a bearer of his deepest wisdom.

The Gospel of Peter tells the story of Jesus's death and resurrection. However, the narrative is told in a way that is strikingly different from the gospels in the Bible. The Bible does not specifically mention the scene of the resurrection itself. Instead, we are only told that the tomb was empty, and later, people saw Jesus alive. The Gospel of Peter paints a cinematic scene where two radiant men descended from heaven and rolled away the stone. Jesus emerged from the tomb, his size almost as tall as a mountain. Behind him was a cross that could walk and talk. The cross was then said to have affirmed that Jesus had already preached to the dead.

Even though some early Christians read and respected the Gospel of Peter, it soon became controversial, especially among leaders of the church. According to the gospel, Jesus remained silent while being crucified—a description that contrasts significantly with the canonical gospels, where he cried out in pain and expressed a sense of both anguish and divine abandonment. This alone caused the early church leaders to question the gospel; the description seemed as if Jesus was not suffering, which fits the idea of Docetism (a belief that Jesus only seemed human). The image of Jesus appearing colossal in size with a talking cross behind him also made Jesus seem more otherworldly. And so, it was decided that the Gospel of Peter was to be excluded from the New Testament. The 2nd-century writer Serapion of Antioch labeled the Gospel of Peter as heretical since it challenged the belief that Jesus was fully human and fully divine.

Almost similar to the Gospel of Mary, the Gospel of Bartholomew survives mainly in scattered fragments. Its contents, however, were considered by many to be more dramatic and imaginative. It narrates the story of Jesus's descent into hell. Although this story was briefly included in the canonical gospels, the Gospel of Bartholomew gives a more vivid account.

The gospel is structured as a dialogue between Jesus and his disciples after the resurrection. In one scene, Bartholomew asks Jesus what happened between his death and resurrection. Jesus responds with a terrifying description of his journey into the underworld, where he preached and rescued the souls there, save for Judas, Cain, and Herod the Great. Jesus allows Bartholomew to take a glimpse of hell for himself. Here, the narrative does not hold back on imagery. There are scenes of angels emerging, demons screaming, and the bowels of the earth opening. Upon seeing this horror, the apostle fainted. Apart from Jesus's journey to hell, the text also includes questions from the apostles about the Virgin Mary, leading to detailed answers about her role and honor in heaven.

These themes undoubtedly reflect the deep interest of some early Christian communities in a grand cosmic conflict and apocalyptic vision. The gospel also echoed beliefs that were popular in Egyptian and Syrian Christian circles, where the descent into Hades was a crucial part of the salvation story. However, like the other apocryphal gospels, the Gospel of Bartholomew was not included in the canon. This was possibly because of its graphic content, theological speculation, and its distance from apostolic teaching as recognized by emerging orthodoxy.

A Hidden World of Belief: The Gnostic Gospels and the Nag Hammadi Library

Scholars were stunned when they heard news of the Nag Hammadi library being unearthed in 1945. They studied each one of the texts, completely intrigued by their diversity and depth. More than fifty works were found—many of them had been completely unknown to modern Christianity. Among them were gospels, revelations, and philosophical dialogues that reflect a radically different understanding of Jesus, salvation, and the nature of reality itself. These writings were thought to be those of the Gnostic Christians, who held beliefs that were different from the teachings of the emerging Catholic tradition.

The Gnostics had a bold claim. They believed the physical world we live in is not perfect but deeply flawed and broken. It is full of pain, suffering, and confusion. The Gnostics also believed that the world was created not by the high, almighty God but rather by a lesser divine being called the Demiurge, whom they viewed as ignorant or perhaps mistaken. Gnostic belief also held that salvation was not about the forgiveness of sin. They believed each person has a tiny spark of the true divine—a piece of the higher, spiritual reality we have forgotten—hidden within them. Forgiveness was not needed to be saved. Instead, salvation came through awakening, by gaining special spiritual knowledge, or *gnosis*, which would help the soul remember its true origin.

The Gospel of Truth and the Gospel of Philip portray Jesus not as a sacrificial savior but as a revealer of hidden knowledge. He spread his knowledge in riddles and parables. This was not to confuse but to guide the soul toward the recognition of its divine origin. The Gospel of Philip provides mystical reflections on marriage, reunion, and resurrection while questioning the literal interpretation of Christian sacraments.

Perhaps one of the most striking Gnostic texts is "The Thunder, Perfect Mind." This Coptic text was written in a poetic-monologue style. It followed a divine feminine figure, who was powerful and rejected, seen and hidden, loved and hated. Scholars suggest it was a way of saying that divine truth is complex and cannot always be put in a simple box. Interestingly, the language in the text felt similar to both the Jewish tradition of wisdom (like in Proverbs) and Christian mystical writings. This shows that in the early days, religious ideas were more fluid compared to the ones we see today.

It is plausible these writings were used by Gnostic Christian sects scattered throughout Egypt and the Levant, which flourished in the 2nd and 3rd centuries. They did not face outright condemnation at first. However, as the church continued to define orthodoxy more clearly, these beliefs began to be seen as dangerous deviations. Figures like Irenaeus of Lyons wrote extensively against them, labeling their gospels false and their theology corrupt.

Some may agree that going through these apocryphal gospels feels like stepping into a crowded room in the early centuries of Christian history. It was a room where many voices spoke at once, each trying to tell its own version of the story. These gospels undoubtedly taught us that the early church had a complex network of communities, each trying to understand what it meant to follow the Lord. These communities emphasized different things. Some focused on hidden wisdom and spiritual awakening. Others spoke of cosmic battles between good and evil, while some talked about the authority of the disciples like Mary Magdalene or Bartholomew. In some circles, Jesus was viewed as a human teacher, while some saw him as a divine being who only appeared physically human. In a few circles, he was both, though understood through different lenses than those eventually embraced by the Orthodox tradition.

It is clear that early Christians often grappled with deep and sometimes uncomfortable questions. Who gets to speak for God? What is the truth, and who decides it? Can women lead? Is salvation about belief, behavior, or something hidden within? The fact that some communities preserved these gospels, despite them being labeled heretical or unorthodox, shows that these questions mattered deeply. And the answers they offered, while ultimately excluded from the official canon, were far from meaningless or foolish. They were reflective of real theological exploration.

These gospels also show that the boundaries of Christian belief were still being drawn. The version of Christianity that became dominant—centered on the four canonical gospels, the creeds, and the authority of bishops—was just one path among several. It won out not only because of spiritual conviction but also through political influence, practical unity, and institutional strength.

Chapter 3 – The Forgotten Apostles: The Quiet Workers of Christianity

It was just another calm morning at the lake. The day was as good as yesterday, so the fishermen spared no time heading into the waters of Galilee. Their hands were already rough with calluses from years of hard labor. Yet, this was the only way for the fishermen to earn a living. They cast their nets into the waters, hoping they could return home with a greater catch than yesterday. Suddenly, a man could be seen from afar, walking along the shore toward the fishermen. At first glance, he appeared rather unassuming, especially since he was dressed similarly to any other Galilean. However, one could feel a sense of deep authority and quiet strength emanating from him. This man was none other than Jesus Christ himself.

"Follow me," Jesus said as he looked at the fishermen.

The brothers, Simon and Andrew, quickly turned to Jesus. They were waist-deep in the water and did not respond right away. However, they could sense something in the invitation. They knew nothing of the man standing by the shore; they had zero interactions with him before this very moment, yet they felt compelled to accept his invitation.

Another tradition has it that Jesus performed a miracle. After preaching from Simon's boat, he miraculously caught so many fish that even the net began to break. This stunned the fishermen around him, as they had lamented before that they had failed to catch anything despite working the entire night.

A depiction of Jesus Christ calling Simon and Andrew to become his disciples.[10]

Regardless of whether they were drawn in simply by his presence or taken aback upon witnessing the miracle, Simon and Andrew quickly abandoned their nets and followed Jesus. The two brothers were not the only ones to have accepted his invitation. The sons of Zebedee, James and John, would do the same. Unlike Simon and Andrew, who were casting their nets when Jesus approached them, James and John were in their boats with their father, repairing their nets. They did not hesitate to accept Jesus's calling. James and John left their profession and their father to become Jesus's disciples. Others followed suit: Matthew, the tax collector; Philip from Bethsaida; and Nathaneal, who was skeptical yet convinced by the promise of something greater. In time, there were twelve men in total. Jesus called them "apostles," which means "sent ones," for their purpose was to carry his message to each corner of the world. And so, through their faith, teaching, and ultimate devotion, the first foundation of the Christian Church was laid.

The Twelve Apostles.[11]

Figures like Simon (who Jesus renamed Peter), John, and Paul—though he was not one of the original Twelve apostles—are among the most famous in Christian history. Their names are often repeated in sermons and sacred texts. Their deeds are known to many believers. Paul, for instance, is revered as the greatest missionary of the early Christian world. He took the message of Christ beyond the Jewish communities and into the Roman Empire. John wrote words that would eventually shape Christian theology for centuries to come.

There were twelve apostles in total, yet only a few names are consistently remembered. What of the others? History is known to favor only a few names while others remain in the background, their stories less frequently told. However, this does not mean that their stories are insignificant. Andrew is often overshadowed by his brother, Peter, yet his journey to spread Christianity to the lands beyond the Black Sea is equally remarkable. Another disciple, Thomas, was a doubter at first, but his faith grew so tremendously that it took him as far as India. These are a few of the Apostles whom many agree were the quiet workers of faith. They went to places where others did not and planted the seeds of Christianity in soil that had never before known its roots. This is the time to remember them.

Andrew: The Apostle of Crossroads

The vast sea was Andrew's friend. Before he accepted Jesus's invitation, Andrew, along with his brother, Peter, had a routine. Every day, they headed into the waters of Galilee to cast their nets. He had been doing this for years, never expecting that his life would change completely. When the man from Nazareth turned to him and extended his hand, Andrew was the first to leave behind his mundane life. This was the start of a journey of faith that would take him beyond these familiar shores.

While Peter's voice often dominated the group, Andrew made his contributions rather

A portrait of Saint Andrew.[19]

quietly in the background. He was not the one who stood on the steps of the Temple and declared the arrival of the kingdom, and he was not the person who wrote letters that later shaped Christian theology. However, Andrew first introduced the disciples to Christ. In fact, according to tradition, he was the one who brought his brother to Jesus, telling him that they had found the Messiah.

Andrew also set the stage for one of Christ's greatest miracles. This episode began when a massive group of people, eager to listen to Christ's teachings, followed him to a remote place. But hunger soon struck them. Jesus was said to have turned to his disciples, asking them where they could buy bread. The disciples hesitated to answer. Philip displayed his concern. They had thousands of followers with them, and he was doubtful they could feed them all, even if they could find a place that sold bread. Andrew, ever the observant one, noticed a boy among the crowd who had five barley loaves and two small fish. Although he knew it was hardly enough to feed everyone, Andrew pointed to the boy.

The offering was inadequate, yet Jesus thanked the boy for his offering. He then distributed them to the people. Suddenly, something extraordinary happened. The food multiplied. No one was left out. Every single person was fed, and they even had plenty of leftovers remaining. Although Andrew's act was simple—he merely brought the boy forward—without his keen eyes, the miracle might not have unfolded in the same way.

Andrew's biggest contributions actually began after Jesus's resurrection. Along with the other Apostles, who dispersed to teach in different regions, Andrew traveled far beyond Judea to spread the gospel. He was believed to have made it as far as Scythia (a land stretching across modern Ukraine and Russia) before journeying into Asia Minor and Greece. In Scythia, his path was far from smooth. Andrew had to face significant challenges in order to spread the teachings of Christ. Not only were the people of the region largely nomadic, but they were also skeptical of foreign teachings. Many resisted his message, yet Andrew persisted. Day and night, he preached among the many tribes, hoping they could see the truth one day. Early Christian tradition recorded that Andrew performed a few miracles after praying in the name of Jesus Christ; he reportedly healed the sick and raised the dead.

Another account recounts his journey to Byzantium. As he entered the Hellespont, a storm suddenly arrived. Andrew prayed that the storm would subside so that he could continue his journey. Miraculously, there was calm. From here on, he continued his mission to Byzantium, eventually founding an early Christian community that would later become the foundation of the Patriarchate of Constantinople.

Andrew also visited a few cities in Asia Minor, including Ephesus and Nicaea. Here, he preached to both Jewish and Gentile communities. He emphasized the importance of unity and encouraged the new followers to remain steadfast in their faith despite increasing Roman hostilities. Of course, his presence did not sit well with everyone. His biggest challenge emerged when he arrived in the city of Patras, Greece.

By the time he arrived in the city, his success was already known by many. People talked about the apostle's ability to pray and conjure miracles for the sick. Many converted to Christianity without hesitation after witnessing him heal the blind and the paralyzed. One time, Andrew was said to have healed the wife of Aegeates, the Roman governor of

Patras. This did not erase the governor's feelings toward the new religion, though. Aegeates saw Andrew's teachings as a direct affront to Roman authority and the traditional pagan beliefs of the empire. In his eyes, Andrew was a disruptor, and his growing influence would sooner or later threaten the empire's stability.

So, the governor ordered his crucifixion. Andrew's last request was to be bound to an X-shaped cross, which would later be known as Saint Andrew's Cross. This was because the saint deemed himself unworthy to be bound in the same manner as the Lord. He died sometime in 60 CE.

The Romans tried to eradicate his influence, yet his memory lives on to this day. Andrew is known as the Protoclete ("first called") in the Eastern Orthodox Church, and he became the patron saint of Constantinople. His presence also reached lands far beyond those controlled by the Byzantines. In Scotland, Saint Andrew was made the nation's protector.

The crucifixion of Saint Andrew.[18]

Thomas: The Apostle of Both Doubt and Faith

The Apostles could be seen sitting in silence. There was nothing but the dim glow of oil lamps lighting their surroundings. The Apostles all wore an expression of grief and fear. They had heard of what had happened to the Lord. Jesus had been crucified. He was gone and buried. While the rest of the Apostles went into hiding, John and Mary remained near the foot of the cross, witnessing Christ's last moments.

A 6ᵗʰ-century mosaic depicting Saint Thomas.[14]

Soon, came whispers of the Lord's resurrection. Mary Magdalene and a few other women went to Jesus's tomb on a Sunday morning, just to find it empty. They went to inform the Apostles of the incident, but they did not believe them—that was, until Jesus himself suddenly appeared before the Apostles who were in hiding.

"Peace be with you," the Lord calmly said to them and showed his wounds.

The Apostles were taken aback yet relieved at the same time. However, one was missing among them: Thomas. The other Apostles told Thomas about Jesus's resurrection.

"Our Lord has returned!" they said to him.

Thomas was skeptical, though. He shook his head and refused to believe his fellow apostles. He told them that he would only believe them if he could see and touch Jesus's wounds with his own hands. He remained doubtful of the resurrection for a week until Jesus finally appeared before him. The Lord told him to touch his wounds and said, "Stop doubting and believe."

Thomas immediately fell to his knees. He was no longer doubtful; in fact, Thomas could feel his faith growing tremendously. He continued Jesus's mission, spreading Christianity to those who were unfamiliar with the Lord's teachings. The Greek Syria-Palestinian historian Eusebius of Caesarea wrote that Thomas spent years spreading the gospel in Parthia (which covered parts of modern Iran and Turkmenistan). Eastern Christian sources also suggest that Thomas might have traveled to Bactria (modern-day Afghanistan and parts of Central Asia), but scholars debate the accuracy of this tradition.

What we can be sure of is that Thomas's next destination was India. According to the Acts of Thomas, the apostle was initially reluctant to continue his mission to India after returning to Jerusalem. However, the arrival of a merchant named Habban changed his mind. Habban was sent to Jerusalem by the Indo-Parthian king Gondophares. Habban's mission was to search for a skilled carpenter to construct a grand palace for the king. According to tradition, Jesus appeared in a vision, informing Habban that he had a slave to sell; he was referring to Thomas. The Lord then appeared to Thomas, instructing him to go with Habban to India. Yet, Thomas resisted. Habban then encountered Thomas, and under divine instruction, he offered three pieces of silver in exchange for his service. The amount is believed to be a reference to the price of betrayal paid to Judas, though the amount is different. Though hesitant at first, Thomas accepted the journey after recognizing it as God's will.

Thomas arrived at Gondophares's court, which was possibly situated in Taxila (modern-day Pakistan). Here, he was instructed by the king to make use of his expertise and build a royal palace. However, instead of using the funds given to him for the palace, the apostle used them to help the poor. He claimed that he was building a heavenly palace for the king instead of one on earth. This enraged Gondophares, who threw Thomas in prison.

However, the king soon witnessed a miracle. Through God's will, his deceased brother was resurrected. He went to the king, informing him that Thomas was not lying. Through his actions of helping the poor, he had indeed built Gondophares a palace in heaven. And so, the king freed Thomas and converted to Christianity.

Now that his mission in northwestern India (Gondophares's kingdom) was done, Thomas made his way farther south. He eventually reached the Malabar Coast (modern Kerala), possibly in 52 CE. The apostle preached among the local Jewish and Hindu communities. Thomas achieved great success in converting many, including high-caste Brahmins and local rulers. From Kerala, he moved eastward toward the Coromandel Coast (present-day Tamil Nadu). Upon arriving in Mylapore (near modern Chennai), Thomas continued his missionary work. However, unbeknownst to the apostle and despite his success, he was also nearing the end of his days.

A stamp with an illustration of Saint Thomas issued by the India Post.[16]

Thomas was said to have crossed the line when he successfully converted King Misdaeus's wife, Queen Tertia, and his son, Prince Ouazanes. When news of their conversion reached the king, he burst into rage. The king saw Christianity as a threat to both traditional religious practices and his authority. He could not accept the fact that his own family had embraced the faith, so he put the blame on Thomas. The apostle was again imprisoned.

This was the end of the line for Thomas, though. He was soon taken to a nearby mountain (possibly St. Thomas Mount near Chennai, India). Here, Misdaeus had his soldiers pierce Thomas's body with spears, resulting in his death and martyrdom. While this version of his martyrdom is more widely accepted, there is another one in which

Thomas was never imprisoned. Instead, the apostle, upon being condemned, fled to the mountain with four of Misdaeus's men in pursuit. The ending is the same. The soldiers managed to catch the apostle and pierced him with their spears until he breathed his last. When Portuguese missionaries came to India in the 16th century, they built a shrine and a church on the site where he was martyred.

Even though Thomas met his fate on that mountain, his influence and legacy in India endured. The people he converted, particularly those along the Malabar Coast, eventually grew into what is now known as the Saint Thomas Christians. While Christianity is not a major religion in India today, the faith has had a long and continuous presence in the nation.

Bartholomew: The Apostle in Shadows

It is quite rare to hear Bartholomew's name being spoken in sermons. Yet, he was one of the twelve men who walked beside Jesus and worked tirelessly to spread the gospel. He is listed among the Apostles, yet we know little of him. Some may say that Bartholomew is a figure who exists in the margins; his presence is felt but rarely seen. Although records of him are scarce, his legacy endures to this day.

A mosaic depicting Saint Bartholomew.[16]

His identity is also a subject of debate. Scholars often identify him with Nathanael, the very man who was introduced to Jesus by the Apostle Philip. Like Peter and Andrew, Philip also hailed from

Bethsaida and was among the earliest followers of Christ. He was often praised for his pragmatic nature and deep devotion. Philip often served as a bridge between the hesitant and the faithful. This could clearly be seen when he first urged Bartholomew to meet Jesus.

"We have finally found the one prophesied in the Scriptures," Philip might have told Bartholomew. "He goes by Jesus of Nazareth."

Yet, Bartholomew remained doubtful. How could someone of great power come from such an insignificant town? His doubts, however, began to disappear upon his first meeting with Jesus. Something unexpected happened. With only a single glance, Jesus recognized Bartholomew immediately. The Lord then made a statement about his character. He called him an Israelite in whom there was no deceit. This left Bartholomew completely astonished. He had never met Jesus before, so how could he know so much about him? His doubt was erased as Jesus continued to talk to him. He referred to seeing Bartholomew under the fig tree before Philip had even spoken to him.

While the exact meaning of this statement is still debated, many agree that it was a deeply personal reference. Perhaps it was a moment of private prayer or reflection that only Bartholomew would have known. Regardless of the meaning, this recognition convinced Bartholomew to become a devoted follower of Christ.

Bartholomew also went on a mission to spread the gospel following the resurrection of Jesus. Although these records are less detailed compared to those of other apostles, ancient tradition suggests that he traveled extensively. It could be plausible that Bartholomew traveled as far as Arabia, eventually reaching Mesopotamia, Persia, and even India. Early Christian writings claimed that Bartholomew carried a copy of the Gospel of Matthew, which he used as the foundation of his teachings.

The spread of Christianity in India is largely attributed to Thomas. However, interestingly, some traditions claim that Bartholomew also played a role in the establishment of Christian communities along the Malabar Coast. Scholars argued that he stayed in India, yet early sources, like those from Eusebius of Caesarea, wrote that traces of Bartholomew's missionary work were found there by a 2nd-century Christian missionary named Pantaenus. This included a Hebrew version of the Gospel of Matthew.

Bartholomew also took his missionary work to Armenia, where he left his deepest mark. It is widely believed that Bartholomew played a role in converting the ruler of Armenia himself, King Polymius, as well as many other members of the royal court. Unsurprisingly, his teachings and success stirred discontent. The king's brother, Astyages, was furious upon learning of Polymius's conversion. He was certain that Bartholomew meant nothing but harm to the nation. Astyages saw the apostle's influence and the faith he introduced as a threat to the kingdom's traditional beliefs.

Astyages planned to remove Bartholomew, not only from Armenia but also from the face of the earth. He ordered his execution. Bartholomew was left with no choice but to go through one of the most gruesome martyrdoms among all the Apostles. He was flayed alive before being beheaded. Fearing that his remains would be desecrated following his martyrdom, tradition holds that his followers secretly preserved his body. Later, his relics were dispersed to different parts of the world. The most significant parts were believed to have been taken to Benevento, Italy. They were then enshrined in the Basilica of St. Bartholomew on Tiber Island in Rome.

Despite succeeding in removing Bartholomew from the kingdom, Astyages failed to put a stop to his influence. To this day, Bartholomew is remembered by the Armenians. They venerate him as one of the apostles who first introduced Christianity to their land. Although his name does not appear often in the pages of the scripture, Bartholomew lives on as the man who carried the light of Christ to distant parts of the world.

James the Less: The Obscure Apostle

Out of all Twelve Apostles of Jesus Christ, many may agree that James the Less is the most obscure. Even his presence in the gospels is minimal. James the Less is mentioned by name in the lists of Apostles, yet his name often appears without any recorded words or defining actions.

The designation "the Less" is far from a reflection of his importance. Scholars suggest that it was likely given as a reference to his stature, age, or perhaps the order in which he was called. While there are traditions that identify him as James, the son of Alphaeus, there is also speculation that he might be the very same James who was a relative of Jesus. Regardless of his obscure story and identity, we can be certain that he was among the twelve men chosen by Christ to spread the gospel.

A painting of James the Less enduring a beating.[17]

In contrast to Peter, Paul, and Thomas, who embarked on a missionary journey beyond Judea, James the Less is often believed to have contributed to the early Christian community in Jerusalem. Remaining close to the heart of the faith's origin, early sources suggest that James had a hand in guiding the fledgling church in Judea. James presumably offered steady leadership to a group facing both external persecution and internal theological debates. This role, however, might have overlapped with that of James, the brother of Jesus. The latter was credited as the leader of the Jerusalem Church, leading to historical ambiguity between the two apostles.

Tradition has it that James the Less preached in regions outside of Jerusalem, with some suggesting he made his way all the way to Egypt to spread the gospel. Unfortunately, his mission here is largely undocumented. There are few surviving records of his teachings compared to his fellow apostles, who typically left behind writings or inspired later Christian texts. Perhaps James's legacy lies in his committed service rather than in his words.

Even accounts of his martyrdom vary according to different sources. While some traditions state that he was stoned to death by the Jewish authorities in Jerusalem following his refusal to renounce Christ, there are other sources that claim the apostle was thrown from the pinnacle of the Temple before being clubbed to death. Although how exactly he died remains unclear, it is safe to conclude that, like the other apostles, James the Less had to pay the ultimate price for his faith.

Chapter 4 – The Desert Fathers: Mystics and Monastics of the Early Faith

There was only silence in the desert. It was not the kind of silence that you experience in a room or even a forest. Here, the silence was deeper or perhaps emptier, accompanied only by the heat of the sun, burning across the endless stretch of the desert sands. According to the gospels, this was where Jesus stayed for forty days and forty nights. He spoke to no one and ate nothing. Jesus faced temptation alone with nothing except his faith.

However, his journey to the desert was not by accident. Almost immediately after his baptism by John, the Lord retreated into the wilderness in preparation for his mission ahead. This time of fasting and solitude was meant to strengthen him spiritually. Jesus knew that before he could go any further, he must confront the temptations that could derail his path. This episode was both a test and a beginning.

A 19th-century painting of Jesus Christ in the wilderness.[18]

Of course, this was not the first time that someone had retreated into the desert looking for a sense of meaning or purpose. John the Baptist had also made the wilderness his home long before Jesus began his ministry. It was said that John lived in solitude. His time was filled with prayers and spiritual preparations. John preached repentance and baptized those who came to him as they sought new beginnings. Centuries earlier, the wilderness saw another figure: the Prophet Elijah. His story, however, was a tad different. Instead of seeking new beginnings, his journey to the wilderness of Beersheba was driven by a conflict. He was fleeing from Queen Jezebel following his confrontation with the prophets of Baal. Fleeing from Queen Jezebel after his confrontation with the prophets of Baal, Elijah collapsed beneath a broom tree. He was tired, overwhelmed, and ready to die. Yet, in that barren place, Elijah heard a gentle whisper from God.

These stories were remembered especially after Jesus's resurrection. The Roman world, in particular, had become more Christian as time passed by. Yet, not every Christian felt satisfied. Some looked at the growing power and wealth of the church with a different view. "This is not what it is supposed to be," these people might have thought. They longed neither for comfort nor influence. Instead, these Christians wanted a real and undiluted connection with God. They wished simply to pray, to listen, and to strip life down to what mattered most. So, they chose to leave the comfort of their cities. With only a little food and a few belongings, they left for the untamed desert surrounding Egypt, Syria, and Palestine, places where prophets and Jesus once retreated to. These individuals who chose the desert over the city were later known as the Desert Fathers.

Saint Anthony the Great, the Founder of Christian Monasticism

In the 4th century, a young bishop named Athanasius of Alexandria penned one of the most influential biographies in Christian history. However, this figure was not a king, a military general, or even a martyr. Instead, it was a man who had chosen to leave everything in his life and go on a journey to seek a better connection with God. Athanasius's work, the *Life of Anthony*, explores the journey of the first-ever Desert Father: Anthony the Great. Unlike other authors and historians who often wrote about figures who lived

A portrait of Saint Anthony the Great.[19]

centuries before them, Athanasius knew Anthony personally. They met during a critical time in church history when Athanasius (who was a staunch defender of Christian orthodoxy) was going against Arianism.

According to the biography, Anthony was born into a wealthy and pious Christian family in an Egyptian village named Coma, located near the Thebaid, sometime in 251 CE. His early life was rather ordinary. One day, a teenage Anthony visited a church and heard a story of a wealthy young man who approached Jesus and asked what he must do in order to achieve eternal life. Jesus's answer touched Anthony. The Lord urged the man to first give up his wealth and care for the poor. Then, he told Anthony to devote himself fully to following Christ. Anthony immediately understood that true riches were not measured by earthly possessions but by a treasure in heaven, granted to those who lived with faith and selflessness.

So, Anthony took the words literally. He did exactly what Jesus told the young man. He sold his property, which was left to him following his parents' death, and distributed the money to the needy. He also left his sister in the care of the pious virgins at the convent before setting off on his journey.

Anthony did not wander too far at first; he actually stayed near the edge of his village. Here, he absorbed knowledge about ascetic life from the local hermits while working to earn a living and alms for the poor. Slowly, he moved farther and farther into the desert. Eventually, Anthony found himself settled in an abandoned Roman fort. He remained there in near-total isolation. Athanasius wrote that Anthony refused to see anyone. He would shut himself inside, spending all of his time praying, fasting, and performing manual labor. He had a friend deliver bread to him twice a year. Otherwise, the saint lived alone. For years, he wrestled with his thoughts, weaknesses, and, as tradition has it, with demons.

Athanasius described Anthony's spiritual struggles vividly. In one episode, he was tested with terrible temptations from the devil. The saint had his mind occupied with thoughts of his former life, doubts about his chosen path, and concern for his sister. The devil also tempted him with lewd thoughts and carnal feelings. However, Anthony succeeded in overcoming these tests. He never stopped praying or meditating on Christ. Whenever he had the urge to give in to the devil's temptations, the saint immediately thought about eternal punishment.

At times, these demonic presences grew extremely intense. They manifested as seductive illusions or appeared as wild beasts and other monstrous creatures. One account retold a scene where Anthony collapsed after being attacked by a legion of demons. He was later found by a friend who quickly took him to a nearby shelter. However, Anthony insisted on returning to the fort.

The torment of Saint Anthony.[30]

That was not the end of his struggles. The demons soon returned, determined to curb his efforts to establish a closer connection with God. Over time, Anthony learned these struggles were not merely hallucinations. They were, in fact, spiritual tests. He knew that the path of holiness was not a walk in the park. Anthony finally learned that escape was not the answer to get away from suffering. He had to confront it.

Therefore, Anthony remained steadfast. He accustomed himself to a stricter way of life. He barely slept, ate very little, and spoke rarely. A normal person would have broken under the weight of such discipline. But Anthony's mind, according to Athanasius, was strong. After two decades of living in isolation in the desert, Anthony achieved a state of stillness and peace, which Eastern Orthodox Christians would refer to as *hesychia*. Anthony reportedly experienced visions, insights, and a profound sense of communion with God. He was believed to have had encounters with angels and moments when the boundary between earth and heaven seemed to dissolve.

His stories of wisdom and holiness reached many, leading them to gather outside his retreat. Anthony never wanted to have followers, but he could not turn them back, especially when they were also on a quest for a deeper relationship with God. So, he took the mantle and guided them. Although he never established a monastery in the way later Christian orders would, Anthony laid the foundation. He taught his followers that prayer was not merely a ritual; instead, it was breath. Fasting was not suffering but rather discipline. Manual labor was far from just a means of survival; it was a form of prayer.

His life was seen as a blueprint for future Desert Fathers. Soon, more figures emerged who adopted similar practices. They would venture out of the safe walls of their cities and live in caves, huts, or small communities scattered across Egypt, Syria, and Palestine. They shared a commitment to spiritual discipline and a belief that the desert stripped away all illusion, leaving only the soul and God.

As for Anthony, the saint remained detached from worldly power despite his growing fame. Emperor Constantine himself had heard of his extraordinary journey. He once wrote to the saint, expressing both his curiosity and admiration; the emperor had recently embraced Christianity, so he was eager to connect with individuals of great spiritual influence. Anthony replied politely but without flattery. In his letters, he reminded Constantine that although he was the emperor, he, too, was still a man who, much like everyone else, was accountable to God. He encouraged the emperor to pursue righteousness above all else.

Anthony left the desert to support Athanasius during the Arian controversy. He assisted his friend in affirming orthodox Christian belief. After his mission was done, the saint quickly retreated to his solitude. He eventually passed away sometime around 356 CE. Tradition has it that he was 105 when he breathed his last. Anthony departed the world without leaving anything behind; he left no written works or even an institution. His only wish was to be buried in a secret location so that his body would not become an object of veneration.

Pachomius, a Soldier-Turned-Saint

Pachomius was born around 292 CE in Thebes. He grew up in a pagan household, so the story of his early life gives no indication of the spiritual legacy he left. By the time he was a young man, Rome was in the midst of unrest. Emperor Diocletian and his successors were persecuting Christians and actively defending the empire's borders. Rome was also in dire need of soldiers. The Roman authorities resorted to forced recruitment. Pachomius was not spared from this. He and many others were conscripted into the Roman army. Pachomius was taken to Egypt, where he was to be trained.

These new soldiers were temporarily imprisoned in a military camp near a city in Upper Egypt known as Tabennisi. This camp was a kind of holding facility where new recruits were confined under harsh conditions before being sent to a garrison. During his time here, Pachomius went through an event that changed his life. While being held in the military camp, Pachomius—and presumably others—were approached by local Christians who brought them food and supplies. They handed these to the soldiers without concern for their status or beliefs. Pachomius was puzzled. Why would strangers show charity to him? After all, he was a pagan and now a soldier-in-training waiting to be deployed to shed blood.

"Our faith in Christ compels us to love everyone. Even strangers who hold different beliefs from us," one of them might have answered.

Although the answer was simple, it left a mark on Pachomius. Even after his military service ended, he could not forget the memory of the Christians' act of kindness. So, he decided to explore the faith. Eventually, Pachomius converted to Christianity and later chose an ascetic life as he moved to the settlement of Shenesit. Realizing that shifting to such a strict lifestyle was not an easy task, he turned to a local hermit named Palamon. Under his guidance, Pachomius learned the ways of solitary asceticism. Fasting, prayer, silence, and manual labor became the core of his life.

Indeed, he followed the example of Anthony the Great and other knowledgeable hermits, but he still felt that something was missing.

What if loneliness is not always the answer to achieving a more personal relationship with God? What if monastic life could be lived together? Surely, it would be possible for a group of men—or women—to live in a community and embark on a path to holiness as long as they were all devoted to the same spiritual discipline. These were probably the questions that lingered in his mind.

His questions were finally answered when he received a vision. Tradition has it that Pachomius saw an angel appear before him. The angel gave him a rule for organizing communal monastic life. Inspired by the divine vision, Pachomius wasted no time and went on another journey. This time, he did not head for an isolated hut or cave where he could be all alone. Instead, he made his way to the abandoned village of Tabennisi, the very same place where he had once been forced to train. He turned this site into his first monastery.

Pachomius only had a small group of followers at the time, but together, they managed to build a structured community, which was divided into groups of ten. A leader would be chosen for each group, who had to report to a higher elder. The monks did everything together. They lived together, worked together, prayed together, and even ate together.

Living in a community, it was a must for each monk to have specific tasks they needed to complete every day. After all, Pachomius put an emphasis on order and discipline. From farming to cooking, from weaving to copying manuscripts, tasks were delegated between them. The monks also refrained from owning any sort of wealth or possessions. They wore nothing but simple robes, ate simple food, and owned nothing individually. Although they were no longer confined to loneliness, they followed a strict rule of life, which included daily communal prayer, manual labor, shared meals, and silence.

Pachomius remained a humble individual, even though he was often praised for establishing the monastery. Despite having experience in the military, where brute strength and force go hand in hand, he led the monks by example rather than force. He was often described as kind and full of wisdom. One time, Pachomius's faith and patience were tested by one of his own monks. He was a novice who got frustrated with the strict rules. He began to insult Pachomius publicly. The rest of the monks expected Pachomius to expel the man from the monastery or at least discipline him. However, Pachomius did neither. Instead, he treated the novice with kindness. He gave him more manageable tasks and spoke to him gently. As time passed, the novice's heart softened. Eventually, he became one of Pachomius's most faithful followers.

As his fame spread, Pachomius received more men who were interested in joining the monastery. When it became impossible for the monastery at Tabennisi to house more newcomers, Pachomius established new monasteries nearby. His sister, Mary, soon joined his path to spirituality. With Pachomius's help, Mary established a women's monastery. This was the first-ever Christian community for women in Egypt. At the time of his death (sometime in 348 CE), Pachomius was overseeing nine monasteries in total. Thousands of monks lived under his guidance. The nuns were led by Mary. They all followed the same rules that applied to his monastery in Tabennisi.

Pachomius refused to be treated as some sort of religious celebrity. He continued to emphasize simplicity in life. He refrained from interfering with church politics despite the requests made by bishops and emperors. Until his death, his concern was only the spiritual well-being of his communities. He preached that holiness was found in the everyday acts of obedience, service, and prayer. The ultimate goal was not to escape the world but rather to sanctify life within it.

Pachomius laid the formal foundation for communal monastic life. His guidance became the basis of later monastic traditions. Soon, his influence was made known even to the lands beyond the Nile. His name became familiar in Palestine, Syria, and, later on, western Europe, where it gave way to the emergence of figures like Basil the Great and Benedict of Nursia. These two would draw from Pachomius's model to establish their own monastic rules.

The Benedictines and Augustinians: Two of the Most Influential Christian Monastic Traditions in Western Christianity

The Eternal City, once seen as the mighty capital of the Western Roman Empire, was crumbling. Chaos was a constant visitor to the city. Its streets, once filled with the footsteps of proud senators and scholars, were now filled with beggars and soldiers. Decadence and corruption could be seen at every corner. Morality seemed to be forgotten. It was amidst this decay that the city saw the arrival of a young man named Benedict. Hailing from Nursia, a small town in central Italy, he had been sent to study in Rome. However, as time passed, Benedict grew discontent with his stay in the city. The state of Rome unsettled him deeply. The city that had once stood for order and greatness now represented everything he despised: depravity, pride, and spiritual emptiness.

Although he was young, Benedict made the decision to leave Rome. He made his way south, eventually retreating into the wilderness near Subiaco. Here, he found a cave near a river, which he called home. For three years, he lived as a hermit, seeking solitude and communion with God. He was nourished only by prayer and some food occasionally brought to him by a local monk.

Soon, word of his holiness began to spread. It reached monks at a nearby monastery. The story goes that these monks had just lost their abbot. In need of a new leader, they approached Benedict and

A portrait of Saint Benedict.[11]

begged him to come to their monastery to lead them. Benedict was never one to desire a leadership position. He hesitated at first.

"My discipline might be too strict," he might have warned the monks.

Regardless of the warning, the monks insisted that he lead them. And so, Benedict agreed. He took up the mantle, and everything went smoothly for a while. One day, though, the monks grew resentful. They were unused to his expectations for order, humility, and prayer. Tradition has it that their discontent grew so intense that they conspired to kill him—the very person they had begged to lead them. One of them secretly poisoned his wine. However, before drinking, Benedict blessed the cup, tracing the sign of the cross in the air above the cup. Suddenly, the cup shattered as if struck by an unseen force. The monks' plan had been foiled.

Another episode recalled a time when a certain priest grew envious of Benedict's holiness. Unbeknownst to him, the jealous priest poisoned his bread. Again, the plan was foiled when Benedict prayed over his meal. A raven swooped down, taking the bread from Benedict's hands before he could take the first bite.

Benedict did not retaliate. Instead of punishing the conspirators, he quietly left the monastery, eventually founding his own monastery in 529 CE. Situated atop a hill at Monte Cassino in Italy, it became the most famous monastery in western Europe. Here, Benedict wrote the *Rule of Saint Benedict.* Many expected it to be a harsh manual or an abstract theological treatise, but it was the complete opposite. The *Rule of Saint Benedict* was practical, measured, and deeply humane. It laid out a daily rhythm of prayer, work, reading, rest, and communal meals. Its motto would later be summed up in two simple words: *ora et labora*, which means "pray and work."

Humility, obedience, stability, and community were at the heart of the *Rule of Saint Benedict.* The monks were also expected to remain in one monastery for their entire lives under the guidance of an abbot. The *Rule of Saint Benedict* also stated that there were seven periods of prayer during the day: Lauds (dawn), Prime (early morning), Terce (mid-morning), Sext (midday), None (mid-afternoon), Vespers (evening), and Compline (night). In addition to these seven prayers, there was also a night vigil.

More monasteries began to adopt this rule, and western Europe saw the early emergence of the Benedictine Order. Benedict himself did not establish any order in the formal sense. However, his rule became the foundation for monastic life throughout medieval Europe. The Benedictines, as they came to be known, followed a rhythm of life that was deeply countercultural. While much of the medieval world was, more or less, violent or unstable, Benedictine monasteries were centers of peace, learning, and productivity. They preserved classical literature by copying manuscripts and maintaining libraries. The Benedictines also worked to educate local populations, cultivate farmland, and provide care for the sick and poor. Their influence spread widely as time passed, stretching from the hills of Ireland to the mountains of Germany. The Benedictine Order also played a hand in recentering the church's focus on spirituality and discipline. They shaped what it meant to live a holy life in a community. In short, these monasteries became spiritual powerhouses that helped rebuild Christian Europe from the ground up.

While Benedict's contribution focused on the communal structure and daily practice of monastic life, another figure from a previous century helped shape the interior life of the Roman Church in a different way. Saint Augustine of Hippo was born in 354 CE in the Roman province of Numidia (modern-day Algeria). Although he was raised in a Christian family (his mother was a devout Christian, but his father was a pagan), Augustine was not baptized. When he grew older, he went on a journey of exploration, spending years searching for truth and meaning. Ever a curious and restless person, Augustine explored the vast field of philosophy and religion until he eventually converted to Christianity at the age of thirty-one. Tradition has it that his conversion was partly influenced by the prayers of his devout mother, Saint Monica, as well as the preaching of Bishop Ambrose of Milan.

Saint Augustine and his mother, Saint Monica.[33]

He was ordained as a priest by 391 CE before finally being consecrated as the bishop of Hippo either in 395 or 396 CE. Augustine wrote extensively. His works, which would shape Christian theology for centuries, include *Confessions, The City of God,* and *On the Trinity.*

One of his biggest contributions was his written monastic guide known as the *Rule of Saint Augustine*. Although less detailed compared to the one written by Benedict, Augustine's Rule also emphasized communal life, the sharing of goods, humility, mutual love, and unity. In his eyes, community was not just practical; it was a reflection of the divine love of the Trinity. His theology eventually shaped Western Christianity, especially in areas such as original sin, divine grace, and the inner life of the soul. Augustine preached that the human heart is restless until it rests in God, and this spiritual longing informed the practices of those who followed him. In contrast to the Benedictines, who helped structure external monastic life, the Augustinians focused on the transformation of the heart through charity and contemplation.

Augustine did not establish a religious order during his lifetime—he passed away in 430 CE when he was about seventy-five years old—but by the 13th century, his story and influence attracted many, especially a group of men and women who went on to organize themselves into communities. These people were known as the Augustinians. They drew heavily on Augustine's theological emphasis on grace and love. Later, this movement split into two major branches. While the Canons Regular of Saint Augustine served as clergy living in the community, the Augustinian friars were responsible for preaching and doing pastoral work, especially in urban centers.

Of course, the Augustinians stayed true to the *Rule of Saint Augustine*, although they adapted it. Where Benedictine life was centered on stability and the quiet life of the monastery, many Augustinian communities were mobile, preaching, teaching, and serving in towns and cities. This flexibility allowed it to be adopted by a wide variety of people. One of the most famous Augustinians in history was Martin Luther, the 16th-century reformer who was an Augustinian monk before he broke from the Catholic Church.

Both Benedictine and Augustinian traditions exist today. While Benedictine monasteries remain as centers of prayer, hospitality, and learning, Augustinian communities are still active in education, pastoral work, and spiritual formation around the world. Although Benedict and Augustine lived centuries apart and took different paths to God, the movements they inspired share a common goal: to seek God in community, humility, and love.

Chapter 5 – Women of the Cross: The Lesser-Known Holy Women of Christianity

Typically, in the ancient world, a woman's place was dictated by rigid social structures. Be it in Rome, Greece, or Persia, most women were confined to domestic roles. Even their identities were tied closely to their fathers or husbands. Of course, there were exceptions. Other than royalty, women could leave their homes to devote themselves and become priestesses. Yet, their opportunities were largely limited compared to men, especially when religious roles were also dominated by them.

Then came the era when Christianity was introduced. The faith spread rapidly among women, offering a radical departure from societal norms. It is clear that Christianity preached a message that was the complete opposite of what had long been accepted. Compared to the rigid hierarchies of Rome or the exclusionary nature of the majority of religious institutions of that time, Christianity preached that all were equal before God. In a world where women's voices were often ignored or silenced, the teachings of Christ gave them a place not only as followers but also as active participants in the faith. They could have a place where they, too, could leave a lasting mark in history.

Women played a pivotal role in the growth of Christianity from the very beginning. In fact, it was women who first witnessed Christ's resurrection. The Gospels narrate how Mary Magdalene, along with a few other women, discovered the empty tomb. Women were entrusted with the message of the risen Christ.

Jesus Christ appearing in front of Mary Magdalene after the resurrection.[38]

Apart from being witnesses to such divine miracles, women were also allowed to become leaders within the early Christian communities. In a time when religious authority was strictly exclusive to males, this was nothing short of revolutionary. Christianity allowed women to lead house churches. They provided financial support for the Apostles and engaged in theological debates. They also cared for the sick, poor, and marginalized, laying the foundations for later monasteries. Popular figures like Lydia of Philippi and Phoebe, a deacon mentioned by Paul, played crucial roles in spreading the faith.

However, as the faith gained more structure and became aligned with the power systems of the Roman world, these early freedoms began to fade away. Women's contributions were gradually sidelined. Nevertheless, their influence was never erased. Many continued to embark on a journey to spread the religion. Some left their legacy as martyrs, others as theologians, and still others as benefactors of the faith.

Saint Helena

Born as Flavia Julia Helena sometime in 250 CE, Saint Helena was said to have had a rather humble beginning. Records are scarce, but scholars suggest that she lived her early life in Drepanum in the province of Bithynia (modern-day Turkey). Since she was of low birth—she is traditionally believed to have been the daughter of an innkeeper—Helena could only dream of a better future. That changed when she met a Roman officer named Constantius Chlorus.

Saint Helena depicted alongside her son, Emperor Constantine.[34]

Constantius was serving under Emperor Aurelian at the time and was sent to Asia Minor as part of the Roman campaign against the queen of the Palmyrene Empire, Zenobia. This was possibly the time when Constantius first laid eyes on Helena; perhaps coming from a humble background himself, he found a companion in her. Other sources claimed that Helena was wearing an identical bracelet to his, which convinced the Roman officer that she was the one for him and that she had been sent by the divine.

It is still unclear whether the two were ever married. Most ancient sources claim that Helena was his common-law wife or perhaps his concubine. Regardless of the real status of their union, the two eventually brought a son into the world in 272. This child of theirs was none other than Constantine, and he would change the course of history.

Helena and Constantius separated when Emperor Diocletian announced Constantius as one of his Caesars. Constantius chose a more politically advantageous marriage, leaving Helena in obscurity.

Of course, had fate been less merciful, Helena's name would have disappeared from the records right there and then. However, history had another path for her, especially when Constantine rose to the throne in 306 CE. The new emperor plucked his mother out of obscurity and bestowed her with the title of Augusta (a feminine form of Augustus, typically given to empresses). Unlike most other empresses in the empire who had their eyes on state matters, Helena—who was believed to have converted to Christianity before her son—chose to get closer to her new religion. Despite having her status greatly elevated, she continued living humbly, dedicating herself to acts of charity. She used her wealth to build churches and help the poor.

She is best remembered for her pilgrimage to the Holy Land. In her later years, Helena made the decision to travel to Jerusalem in search of the sacred sites tied to the life of Jesus Christ. Her intention was pure; she sought to preserve them for future generations. With the guidance of local Christians, she succeeded in locating an ancient pagan temple (possibly dedicated to either Venus or Jupiter) that had been built over Golgotha (the site where Christ was crucified) in the early 4th century. She ordered the destruction of the temple. According to ancient sources, she uncovered three crosses beneath the earth. Identifying which of these was the True Cross was not an easy task. However, a miracle occurred when a sick woman was brought before each of the relics. She was told to simply touch them. The first two did nothing, but when the sick woman touched the third cross, she was miraculously healed. Helena was convinced that she had accomplished her mission and found what she had sought.

The finding of the True Cross.[25]

The discovery of the True Cross was not the only contribution Helena made to the history of Christianity. She also played a hand in Constantine's decision to build the Church of the Holy Sepulchre. This was done to ensure that Christ's burial place and the site of the resurrection would be forever preserved. Helena is also credited with discovering other relics besides the True Cross. She uncovered the nails used in the crucifixion, which she gave to her son; one was placed in Constantine's helmet, and another was installed in the bridle of his horse. Another tradition suggests she discovered the Holy Tunic (also known as the Seamless Robe of Jesus). Helena is also credited with finding pieces of the rope that Christ had been tied with on the cross. This relic is now stored in the Greek Orthodox Stavrovouni Monastery.

Helena spent the rest of her life in service to the faith she held so close to her heart. She eventually passed away sometime in 330 CE with her son, Constantine, by her side. She was buried in a grand mausoleum (the Mausoleum of Helena) outside Rome. Over time, she became one of the most venerated women in Christian history. Though she lived before the Christian Church's formal canonization process began, she was honored as a saint by early Christians and remains highly respected in both Western and Eastern Christian traditions.

The Scholar and the Martyr: The Story of Saint Catherine of Alexandria

Thousands of years ago, Alexandria was considered a jewel of the ancient world. It was a melting pot for not only philosophy and knowledge but also faith. It was also here that Catherine was born in the late 3rd century CE. The exact details of her early life are not clear. According to tradition, she belonged to a noble family; she was possibly of royal descent.

Saint Catherine of Alexandria.[36]

Women of her time rarely received a formal education, which was reserved for men. However, Catherine was given the privilege to surround herself with knowledge. She was trained in an array of fields and subjects, including rhetoric, philosophy, and literature. From an early age, she was said to have possessed a remarkable ability to absorb knowledge; some accounts suggest Catherine surpassed even the most learned men of Alexandria in her understanding of the great classical works. Intellect was her greatest weapon, yet philosophy was not the only thing that captured her heart. As she delved deeper into books and scrolls and engaged in many discussions with scholars, Catherine eventually found herself drawn to something that the schools of Alexandria were not able to offer: the endless knowledge of Christianity.

During her time, Christianity was far from being a popular religion. In fact, this was a time when the faith was seen as a rebellious sect, especially by the Roman citizens. Catherine, however, was believed to have been given a vision, one that changed her life. In this vision, she saw the Virgin Mary holding the infant Christ. Catherine tried to touch the child, but he immediately turned away. This scene did not sit well with Catherine. She immediately sought counsel from the Christian elders in Alexandria. They told her that she should not take the vision lightly, as it was a sign from God himself. The infant turning away from her touch meant that she had not yet fully given herself to Christ.

From here on, Catherine knew she had found her calling. She converted to Christianity and became a devoted servant of the faith. Her path was fraught with peril, though. She was living under the reign of Maxentius, who is remembered as one of the greatest persecutors of Christians before the rise of Constantine. Under the emperor's merciless gaze, those who abandoned the Roman gods for Christianity were seen as threats to the empire. But Catherine was not one who cowered easily.

While other Christian Romans practiced their faith in secret, Catherine boldly showed her devotion. Ancient sources described her confronting Maxentius herself. She challenged the emperor on the persecution of Christians. This bold action could have caused her execution, but Maxentius was probably amused by her audacity. He called upon fifty grammarians (influential philosophers and orators in Alexandria) to debate against her. Unfortunately for the grammarians, Catherine was incredibly talented with words. Using her vast knowledge of both philosophy and theology, she crushed their arguments one by one. Tradition has it that these men were so moved by her words and reasoning that they converted to Christianity. This undoubtedly enraged the emperor.

Nevertheless, Maxentius refrained from ordering her execution. The emperor demanded that she renounce her faith, promising her not only wealth and power but also marriage. These things did not deter her. No longer having the patience, Maxentius subjected her to one of the most brutal forms of execution: the breaking wheel. The emperor expected to see the wheel shatter every one of Catherine's bones. Yet, legend has it that when she was placed upon it, the wheel's deadly spikes flew outward, taking the lives of her executioners instead.

This divine intervention stunned the crowd. Some of them even began to question Maxentius's authority. However, this was the end of the line for Catherine since the emperor wished for nothing else but to see her dead. She was led beyond the city walls, where she was finally beheaded. Tradition described her death vividly. Instead of blood spilling from her wounds, milk slowly flowed on the ground, which many viewed as a sign of purity. Tradition has it that her body was transported to Mount Sinai. Here, a monastery was built in her honor many centuries later. Known as Saint Catherine's Monastery, it is one of the oldest Christian monasteries in the world, and the structure is still being used today.

Partners in Faith: The Story of Saints Priscilla and Aquila

Priscilla and Aquila were of Jewish heritage, and they eventually became two of the most influential figures in early Christianity. Unlike Catherine, their story is not centered around the theme of defiance or martyrdom. Instead, theirs is a story of perseverance.

The two were married and lived in Rome, where they made their living from making tents. Although considered humble by many, this trade was practical since it provided shelter for soldiers, travelers, and merchants. Their lives began to change when Emperor Claudius took the throne following the assassination of his nephew, Emperor Caligula. Sometime in 49 CE, Claudius issued an edict, resulting in the expulsion of Jews from Rome. Both Priscilla and Aquila had no other choice but to leave the once-safe city of Rome. They eventually reached Corinth, one of the Mediterranean's busiest trading hubs.

Priscilla and Aquila were not the only ones who came to the city as a result of the edict. The Apostle Paul had also made his way to Corinth after enduring multiple episodes of beatings and imprisonment for his teachings about Christ. Despite the persecution and rejection, Paul refused to remain silent. Even in Corinth, he continued preaching.

However, in a city best known for its wealth, decadence, and idolatry, he might have struggled to make his voice heard. That was, until he met Priscilla and Aquilla.

The couple welcomed Paul as if he were their own brother. They immediately found common ground, especially with their shared experience as tentmakers. Soon, Paul lived and worked with them. They crafted tents during the day, but their nights were filled with a completely different task. Together with Paul, they spread the gospel and founded the Corinthian church. They remained in Corinth for a year and a half before Paul decided to move on to Ephesus. Priscilla and Aquilla tagged along, but when Paul left again, the couple remained in Ephesus. They established a church in their home. Their door was always open to those seeking the truth.

Saint Paul (left) staying with Priscilla and Aquila.[37]

In Ephesus, the two met Apollos, a Jewish Christian from Alexandria. Although Apollos had great knowledge of the scripture, it was incomplete. He was well versed in the baptism of John, but he had no knowledge of the significance of Christ's death and resurrection. Priscilla and Aquila recognized the potential in Ephesus, so they took him aside and taught him all the things he did not yet know.

The couple eventually made the decision to return to Rome years later, thinking it was safe compared to the era of Claudius. Unfortunately, the Eternal City still had doubts over those who refused to embrace paganism. Nevertheless, Priscilla and Aquila remained in the city. They turned their home into a church. It was a sanctuary for those who believed in Christ despite the threats thrown at them by the Roman authorities. The couple knew the risk was immense. If they were ever caught spreading the religion, death would be their reward.

Their story ends, at least from recorded history, following their move to Rome. While some claim they perished in the persecution that followed, others suggest the two returned to Ephesus after being affected by the Great Fire of Rome in 64 CE. Regardless of their end, Priscilla and Aquila remain deeply influential in the early Christian movement. Paul himself spoke highly of the couple, praising them constantly in his letters. He even credited the two with saving his life.

From Vengeance to Faith: The Story of Olga of Kiev

The Varangians were fierce people. These Norse warriors and traders hailed from Scandinavia and had reached eastern Europe by the 9th century. Although initially arriving as merchants and mercenaries, they were quick to grow their influence. They managed to establish many settlements in the region and took control of key trade routes that linked the Baltic Sea to the Byzantine Empire and the Caspian Sea. As time passed by, the Varangians integrated with the local Eastern Slavic tribes. From here on, they were referred to as the Rus' people.

Saint Olga of Kiev.[38]

However, according to the *Primary Chronicle* (a 12th-century East Slavic historical record), the local tribes were constantly at each other's throats to the point where they struggled to govern themselves. They invited a Varangian leader named Rurik to lead them, hoping he could put an end to their continuous internal conflicts. Rurik accepted the honor in 862 CE, marking the beginning of the Rurikid dynasty. His successors expanded their influence. Oleg succeeded in conquering Kiev in 882 CE, resulting in the establishment of Kievan Rus', the early medieval state that became the foundation for modern Russia, Ukraine, and Belarus.

Olga was born in this state. Her beginnings were far from humble. She was married to a ruler of the Rurikid dynasty, Prince Igor of Kiev. However, when tragedy struck, Olga embarked on a path of vengeance.

The Drevlian tribe had been growing restless under Igor's reign. They were not willing to pay tribute to the prince, yet they relented each time due to the number of escorts he had with him. One day, Igor arrived before the Drevlians with minimal protection. This was the golden opportunity the Drevlians had been waiting for. They captured the prince and put him to death in the most horrible way possible. Legend has it that the Drevlians bent two trees to the ground to the point where the uppermost set of leaves was on the same level as their feet. Then, they tied each of Igor's legs to the trees before letting their forceful return to their natural position tear him apart.

With Igor's death in 945, the Drevlians thought they were a step closer to freedom. They sent envoys to Kiev with a proposal. Their prince sought Olga's hand in marriage. The Drevlians saw this union as a way to solidify their control over the land. However, this miscalculation would cost them greatly.

Olga was not a woman to be trifled with. Yes, she was grieving for her husband, but she was far from being weak. She did not express her anger toward the envoys immediately. Instead, she welcomed them and listened to their offer. Olga told them that she needed a day before she could give an answer. She ordered the envoys to return to their boats for the night. Olga promised them that her people would carry them in their boats—like a palanquin—into her city the next day when she would finally give her answer. Seeing this as a great honor, the Drevlian envoys obeyed.

She kept her word—well, at least half of them. The next morning, the Drevlian envoys found themselves being carried on their boats by the people of Kiev as if they were royals. However, little did they know, they were not heading toward the city but to an open ditch that had been dug the night before. Under Olga's orders, the Drevlian envoys were thrown into the deep pit and then buried alive.

This was only the beginning of Olga's vengeance. Her next step was to send word to the Drevlian prince that she had gladly accepted his proposal on one condition. The princess requested that the prince send his most distinguished men to Kiev so that they could escort her to Iskorosten (the capital of the Drevlians) in a manner befitting a queen.

The Drevlian envoys being thrown into an open ditch.[39]

The prince, who was not aware of the fate of his envoys, fulfilled her wish. He sent his highest-ranking men, the best warriors of all, to Kiev. They were greeted warmly by Olga and her subjects. Treating them like special guests, Olga insisted the Drevlians indulge in a luxurious bath before returning to the matters at hand. The Drevlians obliged, seeing the treatment as an honor. Unfortunately, this was the place where they met their end. The doors behind them were bolted, making it impossible for the Drevlians to escape when the building was set aflame by Olga's men.

Still, Olga was not yet satisfied. Another request was made. This time, Olga planned to unleash another massacre under the guise of mourning for her husband. After performing the funeral rites for Igor, she requested that the Drevlians arrange a grand feast to welcome her into their city. Completely unaware of the event at the bathhouse, the Drevlians in the city obliged. They welcomed the princess and her entourage with open arms and drank late into the night. However, Olga's men were careful not to get intoxicated. The moment the Drevlians became drunk, Olga's warriors slaughtered their enemies. Thousands were said to have been killed.

Olga had one last plan to avenge her husband. With an army, the vengeful princess laid siege to the Drevlians' stronghold. The Drevlians had no intention of seeing Olga's wrath, so they begged for mercy. The princess promised mercy but only if the Drevlians could deliver her a simple tribute: three pigeons and three sparrows from each house. Desperate to save their lives, the Drevlians complied. They breathed easy when they saw Olga's forces retreat, yet unbeknownst to them, Olga had already devised one last horror. At night, the princess had her men tie sulfur and burning cloth to the birds. Knowing that these birds would return to their nests in Iskorosten, Olga ordered them to be released. Flames soon took over the city. Those who did not succumb to the fire fled, only to be captured by Olga's army. Some were killed, others were turned into slaves, and the remaining people were spared with the condition that they pay her tribute.

With her path of vengeance finally at an end, Olga turned her attention to governing. She ruled over Kiev as a regent for her young son, Sviatoslav. While she had been ruthless in avenging her husband, Olga was far from a tyrant. During her reign, trade was stabilized. Another contribution of hers came in the form of faith. Olga was a pagan, but sometime between 945 and 957, the queen received baptism after her visit to the Byzantine Empire. From here on, Olga—using her Christian name Helena, after the mother of Constantine the Great— worked tirelessly to spread the teachings of Christ to her people.

However, the religion was not accepted by all of her subjects. Even her own son refused to embrace Christianity. Being raised in the warrior traditions of his ancestors, Sviatoslav preferred paganism, as he saw Christianity as weak. Olga died in 969 CE without having the chance to see her kingdom embrace the religion, but her influence lasted beyond her death. When her grandson, Vladimir the Great, came to the throne and converted to Christianity, the Rus' people followed suit.

Saint Hedwig of Silesia

Saint Hedwig of Silesia (originally known as Hedwig of Andechs) was born into the noble House of Andechs in Bavaria sometime in 1174. Since this was also a time when the Catholic faith was placed above all else, it is not surprising that Hedwig received a cultured and pious upbringing. Ever since she was young, Hedwig was trained in the expected skills of courtly life, such as the art of diplomacy, estate management, and family alliances. She also learned about her faith. She learned Latin and studied scripture in a Benedictine convent.

Stained glass depicting Saint Hedwig of Silesia.[80]

Despite her extensive education in religion, Hedwig would not become a nun. She was part of a noble family, so she was bound by duty to marry someone who could benefit her family. As a child, Hedwig was betrothed to Henry the Bearded. As the duke of Silesia, he ruled over the fragmented Polish lands.

Yet, Hedwig did not plan on simply existing as a silent consort. After their union, she became Henry's most trusted advisor. She was right by Henry's side, guiding his every decision, no matter how turbulent the situation in Silesia was. Although she was well versed in governance and fluent in court life, Hedwig never left her faith behind.

Despite living in comfort, Hedwig was not afraid to step outside of her palace. She believed that her wealth and status were not for her to enjoy but to use in the service of others. While many rulers saw charity as an obligation of the throne, Hedwig viewed it as a personal duty. It was a must for her to tend to the needy. Hedwig was also credited with founding several hospitals, convents, and churches in the region, which allowed the poor, the sick, and the forsaken to have a place of refuge. Hedwig was always on the move, looking to help her subjects. Even during the harshest of winters, she refused to sit still.

Hedwig was one of the key figures involved in the establishment of the Cistercian nunnery in Trzebnica in 1202. This was the first Cistercian convent in Poland. The convent also served as a place where women could dedicate their lives to God without the traditional expectations of noble marriage. Here, status became non-existent. It was a sanctuary for both widows and noble women alike.

Of course, with great responsibility and status on her shoulders, Hedwig was not spared from suffering. Hedwig's family got themselves embroiled in chaos when conflict arose in Poland. Rival factions fought for control. Henry sought to unify Poland under his rule, but the mission was far from being a walk in the park. Battles took place, and rebellious nobles and rival dukes tried to kill him. These conflicts cost Henry dearly. It was clear that he was nearing the end of the road, yet Hedwig remained by his side.

Hedwig intervened when Henry was captured by his enemies. Using her skills of diplomacy, the duchess was able to negotiate his release. They returned to Silesia after Henry was released, but their test was not yet over. After years of ruling together, Henry finally met his end in 1241 during a battle against the invading Mongol army. With the death of her husband, Hedwig made the decision to take a step back. She renounced the privileges of court life and refrained from meddling in political matters. She chose the path of devotion and humility rather than continuing her journey as a widowed duchess.

Hedwig retreated to the very monastery she had founded in Trzebnica. Although she did not take formal vows, Hedwig lived as one of the sisters. Her life became fully dedicated to prayer and charity. Even during her final years, Hedwig continued to serve the needy and the poor. Pilgrims often sought her counsel, the poor found refuge under her tender care, and the sick received comfort from her hands.

Hedwig passed away on October 15th, 1243. She was said to have departed peacefully, surrounded by the nuns of Trzebnica whose lives she had made possible. Tradition has it that soon after her death, miracles began to take place. Some accounts tell of the sick being miraculously healed after praying at her tomb in the monastery. Others spoke about a divine light appearing over her tomb, which signified her holiness. There were also accounts that talked about visions of Hedwig appearing before those in distress. Even after her death, Hedwig offered people comfort and guidance. Her contributions and these miracle episodes led to her canonization; Hedwig was canonized by Pope Clement IV about twenty-five years following her death.

Chapter 6 – The Gospel in the Far East: Christianity's Journey to China, Korea, and Japan

The caravan could be seen moving slowly across the Silk Road. This was a common sight back then, especially since the ancient routes—spanning over six thousand kilometers—linked China to the West. Traders and merchants would journey along the vast stretches of the routes, eager to make their way to bustling markets so that they could sell their precious goods.

However, there was one particular figure whose goal was not to reach the marketplace. Known simply as Alopen, this Nestorian monk hailed from the Persian Empire and had made the decision to travel to Chang'an (modern-day Xi'an), the capital of the Tang dynasty. The monk brought religious scrolls with him. This doctrine was utterly foreign to the city of Confucian scholars, Buddhist monks, and Daoist mystics.

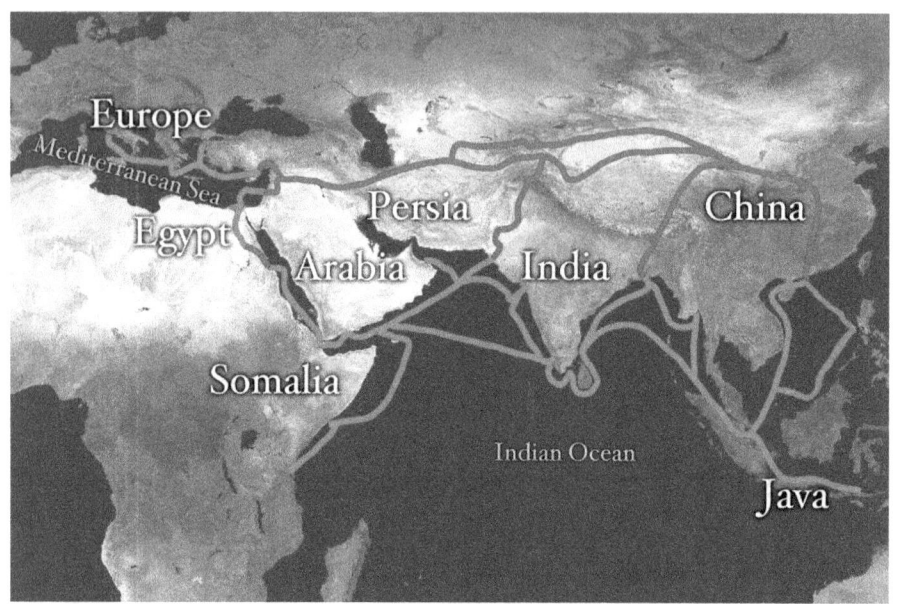

The map of the Silk Road. The red marks the land routes, while the blue marks the sea routes.[81]

Alopen arrived at the imperial court of the ruling emperor, Taizong, in 635 CE. The second emperor of the Tang dynasty, Emperor Taizong, had built a great reputation for himself by bringing China to even greater heights. Apart from expanding the borders of his empire, the emperor was also popular for being open to reforms and criticisms. Alopen was beyond grateful to have been welcomed to the court by an emperor who was willing to listen to his teachings. Emperor Taizong was always curious about foreign knowledge. He ordered the translation of Alopen's texts into Chinese.

Ancient sources claimed that the emperor himself went through the translated sacred texts in his imperial library, studying the foreign religion from top to bottom. Perhaps impressed with the truth of the religion, Emperor Taizong soon issued an imperial edict that allowed the construction of a Nestorian church in the city. From here on, Christianity began to find a foothold in China. To the locals, this religion was known as *Jingjiao* (景教), which directly translates to "Luminous Religion." Nestorian Christianity thrived under the protection of the Tang emperors following Emperor Taizong. For over a century, the religion spread along the trade routes, resulting in the conversion of both elites and commoners.

Unfortunately, this era of tolerance was not meant to last forever. Things went south by the mid-9th century when China saw the rise of Emperor Wuzong. Seeing foreign religions, including Buddhism, as threats to the Chinese identity, the Taoist emperor began to take drastic actions. In 845 CE, Emperor Wuzong played a hand in the anti-Buddhist persecution. Temple lands were taken away, and their wealth was confiscated. Buddhist monks were either forced into lay life or into hiding. Buddhists were not the only ones affected by the emperor's actions. Christians also fell victim to the persecution, along with followers of Judaism, Manichaeism, and Zoroastrianism. Christianity essentially vanished from China, although this erasure was not permanent.

China remained largely untouched by Christianity for four hundred years until the arrival of the Mongols. When Genghis Khan and his successors began carving out the largest contiguous empire in history, China began to see a change in its religious life again. The Mongols were said to have had a unique religious tolerance. Part of their ranks were Nestorian Christians, including Sorghaghtani Beki (the mother of Kublai Khan), who was believed to be sympathetic to Christianity. When Kublai Khan succeeded in controlling China and established the Yuan dynasty (1271–1368), Christian missionaries were once again welcomed into the empire.

In 1294, the Yuan capital of Dadu (modern-day Beijing) received the arrival of an Italian Franciscan missionary named John of Montecorvino. In contrast to Alopen (who had presumably taken the journey to China on his own initiative), Montecorvino was a Latin Christian sent by the pope himself. His mission to spread the faith was met with a few challenges despite the Mongols being relatively tolerant of different religions. The Nestorians had arrived in China centuries before his arrival and had succeeded in building a strong network within the Mongolian court. When Montecorvino introduced the region to Roman Catholicism, which had theological differences from Nestorian Christianity, the Nestorians saw him as a rival. They resisted his influence, with some even going to the extent of spreading false rumors about Montecorvino just so they could discredit his mission.

Of course, the Nestorians were not the only ones who saw him as a foe. Many Chinese elites, Buddhist monks, and Daoist scholars rejected his teachings since they viewed Christianity as a foreign intrusion. Confucian scholars and Daoists, in particular, found Christian teachings to be incompatible with Chinese traditions, especially ancestor worship.

Montecorvino worked alone for over a decade. He had little communication with the pope due to the distance between China and Rome.

Nevertheless, Montecorvino succeeded in making significant progress in his mission. He translated parts of the New Testament and Psalms into Mongolian, allowing Christianity to be more accessible to the local population. In addition to baptizing Mongolian elites and some Chinese people, Montecorvino built a church in 1299. This was followed by another church and a monastery in 1305. Schools were established, where young boys were taught Latin and Christian teachings. They were trained to become future missionaries.

By 1307, Montecorvino's efforts were finally recognized by Pope Clement V. Seven Franciscan bishops were sent to lighten the load on his shoulders, though only three survived the long, perilous journey. A year later, Montecorvino was appointed the first archbishop of Khanbaliq (also known as Dadu, modern Beijing) and given the title patriarch of the East, which gave him authority over all Catholic missions in Asia.

However, the road to spreading the religion was never free from obstacles. When the Mongols fell to the Ming dynasty (1368–1644), the emperors sought to restore Han Chinese rule and erase any trace of foreign influences. Therefore, Christianity faded once more.

Two centuries later, Christianity resurfaced in China when the Jesuits (an order of Catholic priests) arrived sometime in the late 16th century. One of the priests was known as Matteo Ricci. In order to accomplish his mission and successfully spread the teachings of Christ to the Chinese people, Ricci chose a rather clever strategy. Unlike the missionaries before him, the priest refrained from imposing his faith outright. Instead, he immersed himself in Chinese culture. He learned the language and spent endless hours studying Confucian classics. His goal was simple: he sought to win the hearts of China's scholars first before subtly introducing his religion. This allowed him to gain entry into the imperial court.

Ricci's patience bore fruit when Emperor Wanli of the Ming dynasty was willing to listen. Ricci and his fellow Jesuits wasted no time in fascinating the court with knowledge of astronomy, mathematics, and cartography. They introduced Western science to the Chinese and built relationships with high-ranking officials. It took time, but the Jesuits succeeded in gaining their favor, eventually giving way for Catholicism to flourish and welcome new converts.

The Cathedral of the Immaculate Conception, which is considered the oldest Catholic church in Beijing. It was built by the successors of Matteo Ricci in 1605.[33]

However, Chinese scholars soon laid out their concerns; they debated whether Christianity was compatible with Confucianism. There was also the Chinese Rites controversy. Matteo Ricci's approach allowed Chinese converts to practice Confucian rituals, such as participating in state ceremonies honoring Confucius. This was heavily opposed by other Catholic orders, including the Dominicans and Franciscans. They argued that these rites were pagan and the direct opposite of the teachings of Christianity. These arguments went on for decades until Pope Clement XI finally spoke out. Papal decrees were issued that banned Chinese Christians from participating in any Confucian and ancestral rituals. This angered the Kangxi Emperor, the third emperor of the Qing dynasty (1644–1912). In his eyes, the pope was interfering in Chinese traditions and customs. Christianity was banned in 1724. The Jesuits were expelled, and Christian converts were forced to face persecution once more.

Christianity remained underground until the 19th century. During the Second Opium War (1856–1860), China suffered a major defeat at the hands of Britain and France. This resulted in the Treaty of Tianjin (1858), which was later rejected by the Qing government. Thus, hostilities continued. It was only after the British and French sacked the Summer Palace in Beijing that China was forced to comply with their demands. This final settlement was named the Convention of Beijing (1860). This treaty lifted the ban on Christianity. Missionaries were given the legal right to freely spread their teachings across China once again.

From here on, Protestant and Catholic missionaries flooded into the region, setting up churches, schools, hospitals, and medical clinics, many of which remain influential to this day. There was resentment among Chinese nationalists, but this did not stop the missionaries. This period saw a significant rise in Chinese Christian converts, especially among the poor and marginalized.

Another episode of violence occurred in 1850. Famously known as the Taiping Rebellion, this brutal civil war was led by Hong Xiuquan. Claiming to be the younger brother of Jesus Christ, Hong preached a vision of an egalitarian Christian kingdom. He wholeheartedly rejected Confucian traditions and called for the destruction of the Qing dynasty.

Hong Xiuquan established the Taiping Heavenly Kingdom, with its capital situated in Tianjin (present-day Nanjing). Having succeeded in attracting millions of followers (many of whom were discontented peasants), Hong Xiuquan sought to replace Chinese culture with a Sinicized version of Christianity. However, apart from clashing with Qing authorities, the Taiping doctrine was incompatible with the teachings of Western missionaries. This led to a brutal suppression launched by both the Qing forces and foreign allies. Today, the rebellion is considered one of history's deadliest conflicts. It resulted in over twenty million deaths.

The rebellion was eventually crushed, but the Qing government could not sleep peacefully at night; it feared the Christians would incite chaos once more. Due to the treaty signed following the Opium Wars, the Qing dynasty was not able to put a stop to the missionary activities across China. From this point on, Christianity gained a stronger foothold. When the Qing dynasty fell in 1912, it was replaced by the Republic of China. By this point, Christianity was no longer a persecuted faith. The religion grew steadily, especially with the emergence of influential figures such as Sun Yat-sen, the founding father of modern China.

While the rise of the Chinese Communist Party in 1949 led to yet another era of hardship for the Christian faithful, Christianity in China continued to exist. Despite being a minority religion, Christianity has become one of the fastest-growing religions in China.

The Arrival of Christianity in the Land of the Rising Sun

Japan was a land of gods, spirits, and sacred traditions. It was still untouched by the Christian missionaries when China was first introduced to the religion. In the 11th century, the Land of the Rising Sun was controlled by feudal lords known as daimyō. This was the era of samurai, warriors who placed honor and loyalty above all else.

The religious life of the Japanese centered around Shintoism. This indigenous faith focused on nature and ancestral spirits. Buddhism was also a familiar faith to the Japanese. It was first introduced in 525 BCE, and after going through multiple hurdles, it was finally accepted and coexisted with Shintoism sometime in the late 7th century. However, Christianity would not set foot in Japan for centuries; this foreign religion would only be introduced to the Japanese in 1549.

The story began with Francis Xavier, a Jesuit missionary from Spain, aboard a ship en route to Kagoshima. Xavier was not alone in his mission. Accompanying him was a figure known as Anjirō. This Japanese man had a rather dark background. He was accused of murder and forced to flee his homeland. His journey brought him to Malacca (a state in Malaysia), where fate led him to meet Xavier.

Anjirō was said to have become fascinated by the teachings of Christianity. He eventually converted, becoming the first known Japanese Christian. He was then baptized with the name Paulo de Santa Fé. In return for Xavier's teachings, Anjirō gave Xavier valuable insights into Japanese culture, customs, and language. Anjirō also convinced Xavier that Japan was ripe for the gospel. Xavier wasted no time in embarking on a journey to Japan with Anjirō in tow, along with two other Jesuits, two Japanese men, and a Chinese man who had just been baptized.

Upon their arrival in Kagoshima sometime in August 1549, Xavier and his party were able to attract the attention of not only the commoners but also the daimyō of Satsuma Province, Shimazu Takahisa. Curious, the daimyō summoned Xavier to his court. Here, the missionary presented his teachings and gave a good impression. As a result, the daimyō allowed his subjects who were interested in the faith to convert. Hoping to establish a trade relationship with Europe, the daimyō also allowed Xavier to build the first Catholic mission in the nation. This warm welcome only lasted for around a year. The daimyō, perhaps fearing unrest, forbade his subjects from embracing Christianity. Those who were caught converting to the foreign religion were subjected to death.

It is not a surprise that Xavier's teachings did not resonate with everyone. The Buddhist monks welcomed him at first, especially when Xavier used the term "Dainichi" to refer to the Christian god. Unbeknownst to the missionary, this was a mistake; Dainichi was actually the Japanese word for Vairocana Buddha. When he finally realized this in 1551, Xavier began using the word "Deusu," a translation of the Latin word "Deus" instead. He denounced the word Dainichi as an invention of the devil, which enraged the Buddhist monks, who relentlessly created problems for the Jesuits.

Regardless, Xavier never planned on backing down. Instead, he turned his attention to the imperial capital, Kyoto. He hoped to gain an audience with the emperor himself. He knew that if he could get on the emperor's good side, then his mission would go smoothly. Unfortunately, he arrived at the wrong time. Japan was in the middle of turmoil. Historically known as the Sengoku period, this was a period of civil war where rival daimyō fought for control of Japan. The emperor held only a small pinch of real power; the city was actually ruled by warring factions. Xavier was quick to realize this. So, he made some changes in his strategy. Instead of focusing on the emperor himself, he planned to earn the favor of the powerful regional lords.

Francis Xavier remained in Japan for two years and achieved significant success in his mission. After his departure back to India, his successors continued his work. Christianity spread in the decades that followed. More churches, schools, and hospitals began to dot the lands across Japan, especially with the support of welcoming daimyō such as Ōmura Sumitada and Takayama Ukon. The Jesuits were exceptionally skilled in diplomacy. They knew that culture and tradition held a special place in the hearts of the Japanese, so the Jesuits made sure to adapt to their culture as they preached their faith. By the late 15th century, over 300,000 Japanese had converted to Christianity, from influential samurai to feudal lords and commoners.

The tides began to turn in the early 17th century following the unification of Japan under Tokugawa Ieyasu, the founder of the Tokugawa shogunate of Japan. Stability returned to the nation, but the shōgun was cautious of foreign influence. Eventually, the Jesuits were seen as nothing more than agents of European colonialism. After all, the Catholic faith had ties to Spain and Portugal. The Jesuits' increasing presence in Asia alerted Ieyasu. The shōgun feared that if left unchecked, Japan would become a pawn in European imperial ambitions.

In 1614, Christianity was officially banned, and a period of persecution took place. Many Japanese Christians were forced into hiding, but the Japanese authorities had already planned a method to root them out amongst the populace. The citizens were ordered to walk on a fumi-e, a type of wooden block that had a Christian image of either Jesus Christ or the Mother Mary on it. Those who would not place their foot on the holy image were outed as Christians. They were first given a chance to give up their faith. Should they decline, torture awaited them. One brutal method of torture involved pouring scalding hot water from an onsen onto the skin of a Christian. If they continued to resist, these unfortunate people were thrown into the onsen and left to drown.

Like many other kingdoms, empires, and nations, Japan had an episode of chilling persecution. In 1597, twenty-six Christians (six foreign missionaries and twenty Japanese Christians, including young boys) were arrested for their faith. They were first tortured before being marched to Nagasaki to be publicly crucified on a hill overlooking the city.

Although the message was clear—Christianity would not be tolerated in Tokugawa Japan—the Japanese Christians held their faith close to their heart and refused to give up their beliefs. To avoid persecution, they went underground and formed secret communities. Referred to as Kakure Kirishitan (simply translated as "Hidden Christians"), they carried on their faith quietly, avoiding the watchful eyes of the Tokugawa regime. They remained underground for over two centuries.

The Japanese Christians were only able to practice their faith openly in the 19th century. This was the time when Japan was forced to end its isolation and accept influences from beyond its borders. The Japanese soon witnessed the Meiji Restoration in 1868, which dismantled the old feudal order. From here on, Japan began to embrace Western ideas, and with this came the return of Christianity. The official ban was lifted in

1873, resulting in the arrival of more missionaries back into the Land of the Rising Sun. Although the religion was legally tolerated, the Meiji government acknowledged it as nothing more than a minority faith. Shintoism was made the main faith of the nation. Nevertheless, Christianity never completely disappeared from the region. Christian schools, universities, and hospitals continued to be built. They became influential in shaping modern Japan, especially in education and social welfare.

The early 20th century saw the emergence of more influential figures, such as the Protestant thinker Uchimura Kanzō, who worked toward adapting Christianity to Japanese culture. However, another challenge came in the 1930s and 1940s when the nation moved toward militarism. Christianity, again, found itself under scrutiny, especially with nationalism soaring. Christians were viewed with suspicion since they were thought to harbor loyalty

Ōura Church in Nagasaki, known as the oldest standing Christian church in Japan.[88]

to Western powers. During this period, Japan saw the arrest of Christian leaders. This was another era when Christian Japanese had to walk on eggshells. At the end of World War II, religious freedom was restored, and Christians were free to practice their faith publicly.

After all those centuries of hardship, the religion finally found a place in modern Japan. Yet, Christianity never became dominant. It remains a minority religion in the country, with only about 1 percent of the population identifying themselves as Christian.

When Christianity Entered Korea

The story of the arrival of Christianity in Korea was slightly different than that of its neighbors. Instead of being introduced by foreign missionaries who sailed to the region, the religion came into Korea via its own scholars and intellectuals.

By the 17th century, Korea was under the control of the Joseon dynasty. The kingdom championed its Confucian ideals. Buddhism had once been dominant, but when the Joseon dynasty made Neo-Confucianism the state's official ideology, the religion was largely suppressed. Society was structured around Neo-Confucianism, and the Koreans emphasized hierarchy, filial piety, and loyalty to the king. Foreign ideas were typically kept at bay. Due to its unwillingness to embrace or even engage with the outside world, Korea was often referred to as the Hermit Kingdom.

However, Christianity was meant to enter the kingdom's tightly closed doors. It all began when Korean scholars were sent on diplomatic missions to China. Here, they met with the Jesuit priests who had been gaining influence in the Ming and Qing courts. The Korean envoys were exposed to Christian books, which had been translated into Chinese by the Jesuits. These scholars indulged themselves in these books on Western learning, which covered a range of fields. They read about technology, science, and math, which they found interesting. However, they rejected the religious aspects found in these books.

Fast forward to the late 18th century, when a scholar named Yi Seung-hun traveled to China. The son of a high-ranking official, Seung-hun found himself deep into the study of Catholic doctrine. In 1784, the scholar chose to be baptized, becoming the first Korean to convert to Christianity. He returned to his homeland, bringing with him knowledge of the faith.

Yi Seung-hun did not work alone. He was assisted by scholars from the Silhak movement. Although these scholars were Confucianists, they were also interested in Catholicism, particularly its ethical teachings and scientific advancements. They were, more or less, reform-minded Confucianists who sought to correct what they saw as the rigid, impractical dogmatism of mainstream Neo-Confucianism in late Joseon Korea. With their help, Yi Seung-hun was able to spread Christianity, first targeting the Korean elite. After baptizing some of them, they formed secret Christian communities since the religion was not yet acknowledged publicly. Despite being accepted in the shadows, Christianity continued to grow. By the time a Chinese missionary named James Zhou Wenmo arrived in late 1794, Korea was already home to several thousand Catholics.

Eventually, this new faith attracted suspicion from the Joseon authorities. Christianity rejected ancestor worship, which was a crucial element of Korean Confucianism. The religion also promoted the idea of equality before God, which was clearly against the rigid class hierarchy of the Joseon society. The Joseon authorities, particularly King Sunjo, concluded that Catholicism was a direct threat to the kingdom's stability.

The year 1801 was a dark time for Christians in Korea. Thousands of Christians were arrested and executed. Seeing the increasing persecution, a Catholic scholar named Hwang Sayong secretly wrote a letter to the bishop of Beijing. He asked for European intervention, hoping it could help protect the Korean Christians. This letter was discovered by the Joseon authorities. As a result, Hwang was tortured and beheaded. From here on, extreme purges were carried out by the government, removing the believers one by one. In 1836, French priests from the Paris Foreign Missions Society managed to secretly land in Korea; this was the first time foreign missionaries had arrived in the kingdom.

Unfortunately, even these priests were not spared from the terror. Bishop Laurent Imbert, for instance, was arrested and executed during the persecution of 1839. Another brutal wave of martyrdom occurred in 1866 under the order of regent Heungseon Daewongun, who ruled in the name of his young son. This anti-Christian campaign took the lives of over eight thousand Catholics. They were all killed in mass executions. The first Korean priest, Saint Andrew Kim Taegon, also perished; he was beheaded at the age of only twenty-five in 1846.

The Korean Christians began to see the light at the end of the tunnel by the late 19th century, when Korea was no longer able to maintain its strict policy of isolation. Following the rapid modernization during the Meiji Restoration, Japan focused on expanding its influence across East Asia. Its main target was Korea, which they saw as a strategic buffer zone between Japan and China. Warships were launched to Korea in 1875, which ignited the Ganghwa Island incident. This was when Japanese forces clashed with Korean troops.

After suffering defeat at the hands of the Japanese, Korea was forced to sign the Treaty of Ganghwa in 1876. With its isolation policy now effectively ended, the Joseon dynasty was left with no choice but to open its ports to foreign trade, beginning with Japan. This openness gave way for Protestant missionaries to set foot in Korea. The influential American Presbyterian missionary Horace Allen was among those who arrived in Korea in the 1880s. As a doctor, Allen earned a reputation for his medical skills. He succeeded in earning favor with the Korean royal court, allowing him to establish Korea's first modern hospital, known as Jejungwon, in 1885. This was a center for both medical treatment and Christian evangelism.

Soon, Korea saw the emergence of many more important Christian figures. Horace Underwood (Presbyterian) and Henry Appenzeller (Methodist) came to Korea, bringing with them Western education, printing presses, and, of course, new churches. In contrast to the Catholic missionaries who focused on the elite, these Protestant missionaries paid attention to the common people.

Christianity became intertwined with the nation's struggle for independence. When Japan took full control over Korea in 1910, Christians actively resisted the Japanese. A major protest against the Japanese occupation took place in March 1919, which was led by the Christian Koreans. Unfortunately, the protest ended badly. Many died, including a young activist named You Gwan-sun. Not only was she tortured, but the activist was also killed for her role in the movement. The Japanese even went to the extent of forcing Shintoism on the Koreans. Many resisted this and secretly continued their own religious practices.

After Japan's defeat in World War II, Korea was finally liberated. From here on, Christianity grew even stronger, particularly in South Korea. The same could not be said of North Korea. When the country was divided, North Korea became a communist state. Christianity was greatly suppressed there.

Myeongdong Cathedral in Seoul, Korea's first Gothic-style Catholic cathedral and the seat of the archbishop of Seoul.[54]

The majority of South Koreans today do not identify themselves with any religion. However, Christianity is considered one of the most influential religions in the country. Almost 29 percent of the population identifies as Christian (split between Protestants and Catholics). Interestingly, South Korea is now considered one of the world's leading missionary-sending nations. Korean missionaries have been sent to many countries across Asia, Africa, and the Middle East. The capital city of Seoul is home to some of the largest churches in the world; believe it or not, Myung Sung Presbyterian Church is the largest Presbyterian church in the world.

Myung Sung Presbyterian Church, the largest Presbyterian church in the world. [35]

Chapter 7 – Faith on the Fringes: Christianity in the Celtic Lands

The dark night was pierced by the sight of a fire crackling in the center of a stone circle. Around it stood cloaked figures. Then, a Druid, dressed in his white robe, stepped forward. His back was facing the great standing stones, each carved with symbols. A boy was being initiated tonight. His eyes were filled with confidence and a glint of fear. In his hands, the boy held a sprig of oak. He was expected to make offerings to the gods, binding him to the tribe and to the old ways.

This was a common scene in Celtic lands long before the arrival of the cross. For centuries, religion was not a matter of creed or sacred books. Instead, it was of earth and sky, of memory and ritual, and of the celebration of their ancestors. To them, the divine was far from unreachable; it moved through the wind and was carried along the streams and rivers. Their stories were often told beside fires. The Celts also looked up to the Druids. They had responsibilities similar to those of priests, judges, and scholars, making them the leaders of spiritual life.

The Celts did not separate the spiritual from the natural. Festivals like Beltane, where they celebrated the coming of summer, or Samhain, which marked the end of the harvest and the start of the new year, all tied time to the land. In their eyes, every well was inhabited by a spirit, and every tree was capable of whispering secrets. It is clear that worship was woven into life itself.

However, despite being on the fringes of Roman influence, these lands would soon feel the winds of change. Traders who arrived on the shores began spreading word of a new god. They talked about a crucified man who had risen from the dead. His sign was neither an oak tree nor a stone but rather a wooden cross. They spoke about his followers who preached nothing but love and salvation. Initially, these stories were passed around in a hushed tone; they were nothing more than whispers among merchants, wandering travelers, and slaves. It would not be long before this new faith took root.

Saint Patrick's Mission in Ireland

The land that Patrick returned to was the same one where he had once been held as a slave.

When he was a boy, Patrick had a rather comfy life. Born in Roman Britain, he was the son of a Christian deacon. Yet, some sources suggest that he did not believe in Christ when he was young. His life changed one day when Irish raiders arrived. Patrick was only sixteen when he was torn from his home. He was taken by the raiders across the sea. When the ship docked in Ireland, he was sold into slavery.

Patrick found himself serving under an Irish king named Miliucc. He spent years tending sheep in the loneliness of the Irish hills. It was also here that he began experiencing his religious awakening. Despite not believing in Christ at the time, he tried praying. He initially doubted the Lord's salvation; he was not even sure which god he believed in. Yet, despite his doubt, he immediately felt as if he was closer to God. From here on, Patrick sought communion with him day and night through prayer.

Six years later, Patrick was said to have received a vision, telling him that he would soon return to his homeland and that a ship was already waiting for him. He escaped his master the next morning and traveled for about two hundred miles to the coast, where he found a ship. Tradition has it that the captain of the ship rejected him at first. However, by God's will, he changed his mind, allowing Patrick to board and leave Ireland. The trip was arduous, but Patrick endured and made it back safely to his homeland.

Slemish in Northern Ireland, believed to be where Saint Patrick once served as a shepherd.[86]

Despite being free at last, Patrick found it difficult to settle back into his old life. All those years in the lonesome wilderness, praying to God day and night, had shaped him into a different person. He could feel himself gradually disconnecting from the Romanized Britons. Plus, he had already lost several years of education. Regardless, Patrick had no intention of leaving the city with which he was familiar.

One day, he experienced multiple visions. In one of the visions, he heard the voices of the Irish people calling to him.

"Come and walk among us once more,"

Patrick did not take the vision seriously at first. But when his nights were haunted by visions that increased in both frequency and intensity, he decided to heed the message. He spent some time in theological training and soon crossed the sea again. This time, he went to Ireland not as a slave but as a missionary.

His arrival was not welcomed by everyone. The chieftains of Ireland were powerful, and the Druids still held sway over spiritual life. They saw Christianity as a foreign faith, and in their eyes, foreign things were not to be trusted. However, Patrick did not step onto the shores with armies or swords. Instead, he came with a message and planned on spreading it with patience. It took time, but his patience eventually bore fruit.

Stained glass depicting Saint Patrick preaching to Irish kings.[87]

He traveled across the island, sometimes alone or with a small group of companions. He never complained when he had to walk through the rain-soaked forests. He never cowered when he stood before kings. His teachings were sometimes ignored. Other times, he was forced to face threats. Patrick endured beatings and was thrown into prison more than once. Because of his teachings, he was in constant danger. Yet, the saint persisted. He believed that the Irish people were ready for change. He believed that sooner or later, they would embrace the faith. Patrick was wise to teach the people that this foreign faith was not something that would replace their world but rather fulfill it. He spoke of a single God who was not bound to a single tree or a stream but was present in all creation. He even used symbols they knew, like the three-leafed shamrock, to explain the Christian Trinity.

Over time, Irish hearts began to shift. Patrick baptized new believers, ordained clergy, and founded churches. He was able to build relationships with local leaders and win over clans. Old festivals and celebrations continued across the island, but they were reinterpreted through the Christian lens. Patrick was well aware that the souls of people could not be changed by force. It could, however, be guided gently, like a river changing course. His mission continued for decades. By the time of his death in 461 CE, Christianity had already begun to weave itself into the fabric of Irish life.

The Exiled Monk: Saint Columba and the Soul of Scotland

When people imagine a monk, they often picture a gentle figure. Perhaps a humble man cloaked in wool, head bowed in prayer, as he moved silently between stone walls. And often, that image is true. Across early medieval Ireland, monasteries were places of learning, faith, and labor. Monks would spend years copying texts, word by word and line by line. While some worked on sacred scriptures, others worked on preserving the wisdom of ancient Rome and Greece. Copying texts may sound like an easy, simple task, but, in reality, it could take months or even years for a monk to complete one manuscript, especially when they were adorned with intricate details like decorative spirals and knotwork.

Saint Columba was far from being a quiet monk. Some describe him as passionate, ambitious, and, at times, uncompromising. He was a man of prayer and faith, but he was also a monk who once rode into battle.

The conflict that eventually led to his exile began when he got into a dispute with another influential monk, Saint Finnian of Movilla. The story, as passed down through Irish tradition, says that Finnian returned from Rome, bringing with him a rare Book of Psalms. Upon hearing this, Columba was immediately fascinated. He took the book without Finnian's knowledge and secretly made a copy. When Finnian discovered this, he was furious. After all, the monk had brought the book at great cost and effort. He demanded that both the book and the copy be returned to him. Columba refused to do so.

The matter was then taken to High King Diarmait mac Cerbaill. He argued that since the book was considered his property, any act of copying it was not allowed; this was one of the earliest copyright trials in history. The king ruled against Columba, famously declaring, "To every cow its calf, to every book its copy."

This dispute did not end there. Unwilling to back down, Columba chose violence. He rallied his clan in protest. The conflict escalated into the Battle of Cúl Dreimhne around 561 CE, with Columba personally leading his men. Although Columba emerged victorious, the battle was won at a terrible cost. Many lives were lost.

Columba, finally realizing what he had started, was wracked with guilt. He also had to face pressure from the church and local kings. They told him to go into exile for his wrongdoings, but the monk resisted. He made his way to a remote island off the northwest coast, known as Inishmurray. Here, Columba sought the counsel of his confessor, Saint

Molaise, who stayed in a monastery he founded there. After listening to Columba's story, Molaise affirmed the decision made by the church and the local kings. He then gave Columba a penance. Columba would not find peace unless he converted as many souls to Christianity as the number that perished in the battle.

Finally accepting his path, Columba left his homeland. Accompanied by twelve disciples, he crossed the sea aboard a small vessel made of wicker and hide. He had no destination; Columba simply wished to go to a place where he could not spot home. Eventually, he landed on the island of Iona. Located off the western coast of Scotland, it fit his plan— the island was so distant that he could no longer see the shores of Ireland.

Almost immediately, he began working on redeeming his guilt. In 563, Columba built a monastery on the island. It appeared rather humble, with its small cluster of stone and timber cells. Yet, this very monastery would become one of the most influential Christian centers in the Celtic world. Of course, spreading a teaching that goes against the land's pagan beliefs was challenging. The Picts held fast to their ancient ways. They carved mysterious symbols into stones and worshiped in groves untouched by axes or fire. But Columba's teachings found a place in their hearts when he made it clear that he did not wish to tear down their ancient traditions. Instead, he wanted to walk beside them.

It was said that Columba made it to the court of King Bridei at Inverness. Here, his boldness won respect. One tale tells of Columba approaching the gates, only to find them barred. Not one to back down easily, he traced the sign of the cross against the doors. Much to the surprise of many, the doors flung open. There is also a story that talks about another one of Columba's miracles. This time, it involved a certain beast in the River Ness. Believed to be the same creature as the famous Loch Ness Monster, Columba was said to have bravely commanded it to flee after lunging at a man. He did so after making the sign of the cross. The beast, adhering to his command, fled at once, never to be seen again. Whether fact or hagiography, the message from these miracles was clear: under God's will, Columba had a power that surpassed both kings and Druids.

Saint Columba converting the Picts.[88]

Columba's faith was intense and disciplined. He lived rather simply. At dawn, the monk would rise and pray. Then, he would go and work with his hands before using the rest of his time transcribing sacred texts. Despite this, he was far from a quiet recluse. Columba was viewed as a leader, and under his guidance, Iona transformed into a force for Christianity throughout Dál Riata and beyond. The monastery and, later, the Benedictine abbey would serve as a pilgrimage site. Monks flocked to this site to seek the blessing of Saint Columba. Then, they would journey outward, carrying books wrapped in leather, crosses carved from driftwood, and a message forged in both fire and forgiveness.

Saint Columba died sometime around 597 CE. His loss was felt far beyond Iona. His abbey outlasted kingdoms, but it was not entirely protected from history. Two centuries after his death, Iona became a victim of the Viking raiders, marking the start of a new and violent era for the Celtic Christian world.

The Gentle Flame: Saint David and the Spirit of Wales

The mountains of Wales were not easily tamed. Still, Christianity did not spread across this land through fiery wars of kings' conversions. Instead, it spread quietly, carried by a man whose life mirrored the very land he traversed: rugged, steadfast, and humble.

Known simply as David, this saint was born into a noble family in the southwestern region of Ceredigion. Since he was the grandson of Ceredig ap Cunedda, the king of Ceredigion, David had royal blood running through his veins. Interestingly, even his birth was—at least according to legend—marked by divine signs. The story holds that his mother, Saint Non, gave birth to him on a cliff above the sea in Pembrokeshire when a storm was raging. Today, the place where she delivered her child can still be visited. It is now marked by the ruins of the Chapel of St. Non. One can find a holy well nearby, which is believed to have healing powers.

The ruined Chapel of St. Non.[89]

David was raised in faith, so it was not surprising that he embraced a monastic life. He is credited with the foundation of a monastery at Glyn Rhosyn. David and his monks adhered to a strict and austere rule. They plowed their fields using their hands rather than oxen. They also refrained from consuming meat and beer. David ate a diet of only leeks and water, a tradition that many believed became a symbol of Wales later on. Despite being born into a royal family, David was at peace living with minimal comfort.

Perhaps it was because of this austere lifestyle that his influence began to grow. His discipline became the talk of the town. His kindness and generosity, along with his healing talents and deep wisdom, were acknowledged by the locals. The saint was believed to have brought a dead boy back to life one time by splashing the child's face with tears. He was also said to have invoked the power of God to restore a blind man's sight.

Of course, the saint did not remain in his monastery all the time. David traveled across Wales, founding more churches and monastic communities along the way. His gentle example was one of the reasons followers came to him from the valleys and hills. His reputation for holiness and wisdom eventually led to his invitation to the Synod of Brefi. Held in the village of Llanddewi Brefi in the 6th century, this church council was to address growing concerns about heretical teachings by a controversial figure named Pelagius. They saw these teachings as a challenge against orthodox Christian belief, and over time, they caused confusion among both clergy and laypeople alike. Church leaders from across the region gathered at this synod. However, David was not included initially, as he was not considered a central figure in the church hierarchy at the time. However, when they found it difficult to bring peace to the assembly, a few of them suggested his name.

David, ever humble in nature, was reluctant to attend the synod. But after being persuaded by his peers, the saint agreed to attend. During this time, another miracle took place. He stood to address the crowd, but some were complaining that they could not see him or hear his voice clearly. Suddenly, the ground beneath him rose into a small hill. David was lifted high above the crowd so that everyone could see and hear him. Then, a white dove came flying by and settled on his shoulder. His speech was said to have impressed everyone, including the senior bishop, Saint Dubricius. David was declared the archbishop of the Welsh Church following this event.

Of course, David's journey was not limited to Wales. He was believed to have made a pilgrimage to Jerusalem, where he was consecrated as a bishop. He then returned home, bringing with him a sacred stone. This relic was placed on the altar of what would become St. Davids Cathedral, which was built on the very site of his original monastery. To this day, the cathedral remains one of the most sacred Christian sites in Wales.

David passed away around 589 CE. His legacy is remembered every March 1st, with hymns, daffodils, and the phrase attributed to him in his final sermon: "Do the little things."

The Integration and Monastic Life in the Celtic World

In comparison to the Roman Church, which centered its authority in cities and dioceses, Celtic Christianity focused more on monasticism. Across the region, monasteries flourished as not only religious centers but also as towns full of spirit and scholarship. These spiritual communities were accepted by the locals because they found stability, education, and refuge there. Abbots and abbesses also held more authority than bishops. Abbess Brigid of Kildare, for instance, sealed her role in the history of Christianity after rising to lead double monasteries that housed both men and women. Considered one of Ireland's three national saints—alongside Patrick and Columba—Brigid guided the people not only in prayer but also played a hand in politics and diplomacy.

Celtic monasticism gave birth to the Book of Kells. It was believed to have been created by the monks at Iona sometime in the 9th century and possibly completed at Kells in Ireland following raids by the Vikings. This handwritten manuscript contains the four Gospels of the New Testament. Written in Latin, it is intricately decorated with a fusion of Christian themes and vibrant Celtic artistry. Each of the pages is alive with impressive knotwork, spirals, and symbolic animals. It was clear that this illuminated manuscript's beauty was made to glorify God. Today, this masterpiece can be found at the Library of Trinity College in Dublin. It is one of Ireland's most precious treasures.

A Dispute Over Calendars: Celtic Christianity Meets Rome

For years, the monasteries of the Celtic world thrived quietly. However, conflicts arose when the Celtic and Roman worlds were brought closer together. Many realized that not all Christians were practicing their faith in the same way. The tonsure worn by Celtic monks was quite different from the one worn by Roman monks. While the latter shaved a circular area on the top of the head, leaving a ring of hair around it, Celtic monks shaved the front of their heads from ear to ear. There was also the matter of ecclesiastical structure. While Rome emphasized hierarchical order, with bishops serving under the pope's authority, the Celtic Church was more decentralized. In these regions, abbots held more power than bishops, given their monastic roots.

A more serious difference was the dating of Easter. The Romans calculated the day of Easter using the Alexandrian method, which fixed the date based on the spring equinox and the full moon. This ensured that it remained aligned with the broader liturgical calendar and the timing of Passover. The Celtic Church, on the other hand, favored an older method that was likely inherited from early Christian communities in Gaul or Britain. This particular method used a completely different lunar cycle, often resulting in Easter falling on a separate Sunday.

These differences came to a head in an episode that took place in 7th-century Northumbria, a kingdom caught between both worlds. Its ruler, King Oswiu, was a Christian convert who was raised in the Celtic traditions. His wife, Queen Eanflæd, was accustomed to Roman traditions. Because of the differences in their traditions, the royal household found itself celebrating Easter on different days. One court would be fasting for Easter while the other was already feasting. This was more than just an inconvenience; it was a public contradiction.

King Oswiu knew he had to resolve the matter. In 664 CE, he called for a gathering at Whitby. This synod was held to decide, once and for all, which Christian tradition the kingdom would follow. Monks, bishops, and nobles filled the abbey founded by Hilda of Whitby, a respected leader and mediator. The atmosphere was thick with tension. Yet, the people knew this matter must be resolved as soon as possible if they hoped to see unity and peace once more.

The Celtic delegation, including Bishop Colman of Lindisfarne, could be seen standing on one side. With a voice full of confidence, he spoke of the traditions passed down from Saint Columba and the Celtic Church. On the other side, one could find a passionate advocate of Roman practice who went by the name Wilfrid. He was said to have appealed to the authority of Saint Peter, the keeper of the keys to heaven. After hearing from both sides, King Oswiu was left with the decision. He stopped to think for a while before finally letting his people know his stance.

"It is unwise for me to go against the gates of heaven," he might have said.

His decision was clear. King Oswiu sided with Rome. Northumbria would follow Roman practices. Decades later, the rest of Britain and eventually Ireland would follow suit. The unique customs and monastic independence that had once flourished in the lands of Ireland, Scotland,

and Wales gradually faded as Roman traditions took hold. Regardless, traces of the old ways still remain. It still lingers in their art, music, and, most importantly, in the memory of the saints who walked across the land to spread the faith.

Chapter 8 – Christianity and Islam: The Survival of Christian Communities After the Muslim Conquest

An army could be seen gathering on the rocky northern coast of Morocco. The spring of 711 was about to be bloody, as a series of wars was clearly on the horizon. This particular army was led by a Berber general named Tariq ibn Ziyad, who commanded under the authority of the Umayyad Caliphate. They had just reached the Strait of Gibraltar. Across its narrow waters lay their target: the Iberian Peninsula, which was, at the time, ruled by the Visigothic King Roderic.

With approximately seven thousand horsemen, Tariq crossed the strait, eventually landing near a large mountain, the one that would bear his name, Jabal Tariq (also known as the Rock of Gibraltar). Later Islamic sources state that Tariq made a special order to his troops upon disembarking from their ships.

"Burn all of our ships," he might have said. This move was thought to be a symbolic gesture. By destroying their ships, Tariq was clearly saying there would be no retreat. The only choice was to move forward or perish in battle.

The Visigothic kingdom was in the midst of turmoil. Although King Roderic succeeded in claiming the throne following a contested succession, he found himself struggling to unite the divided nobility. Dissatisfaction and rivalries plagued the kingdom. Some even saw the arrival of the Muslim troops as good news; they planned on using the invasion as an excuse to weaken Roderic's hold.

Meanwhile, Tariq's forces wasted no time in advancing inland. His army eventually met Rodric's forces near the Guadalquivir River. Roderic's forces were larger in number—perhaps twice the size of Tariq's men—but they did not possess what the Muslims had at that time: unity and discipline. Despite outnumbering Tariq and his forces, the Visigoths were defeated. Roderic was killed in the battle.

A 15ᵗʰ-century manuscript depicting Tariq ibn Ziyad (right) and Visigothic King Roderic.⁴⁰

Their victory at the Battle of Guadalete allowed the Muslims to advance with surprising speed. After fighting off a small garrison, they managed to take Córdoba before pushing into central Hispania. Their main goal was to reach the Visigothic capital, Toledo. Along their way, many cities chose to open their gates peacefully. While some wished to avoid bloodshed due to the lack of organized defense, others hoped they could secure favorable terms. Later on, Tariq received reinforcements from North Africa, led by Musa ibn Nusayr. This swelled their number to at least twelve thousand. Even though the two commanders did not always see eye to eye, they succeeded in subduing key regions, including Zaragoza and Mérida. By 718, the Muslims had already laid firm foundations of what would become al-Andalus.

However, Spain was not the first region to experience the expansion of Muslim rule. Rather, it was the westernmost edge of a movement that had reshaped the political map of the Middle East and North Africa. The first few steps of expansion took place after the death of the Prophet Muhammad in 632 CE. Leadership was then passed to his close companion, Abu Bakr, who went on to become the first caliph in what would be known as the Rashidun Caliphate. Under this caliphate, the Muslim community began to strengthen its influence further.

The Middle East was the first to witness the spread of Islamic influence. In just a few years, the Muslims were able to confront two colossal powers: the Byzantine Empire and the Sasanian Empire. Under Khalid ibn al-Walid, a series of campaigns was launched in 633 CE against the Sasanians, culminating in the Battle of al-Qadisiyyah in 636, which opened the door to the conquest of Iraq. The Muslims advanced, capturing the Sasanian capital, Ctesiphon, later on. The empire collapsed entirely by 651, with its last ruler, Yazdegerd III, assassinated while he was on the run.

The Battle of Yarmouk in 636 saw the Muslim forces decisively defeat the Byzantines in Syria. Soon after, Damascus fell, followed by Emesa and other key cities. Meanwhile, Jerusalem surrendered in 638 without any bloodshed. Caliph Umar himself entered the city and agreed to a peaceful handover, walking alongside the Christian patriarch, Sophronius. Next was Egypt, yet another region under the control of the Byzantines.

A campaign into the Nile Valley was launched in 639, with Amr ibn al-As commanding the Muslim army. Since the Byzantines were already weakened, the empire was unable to maintain a strong defense. This left Egypt vulnerable. The Byzantines met the Muslim forces at the Battle of Heliopolis in 640. However, the Muslims were a force to be reckoned with. The Byzantines were defeated, allowing the Muslims to march deeper into the Nile Delta. Alexandria, Egypt's major port city—and the last major Byzantine stronghold—was captured in 642, completing the Muslims' conquest of Egypt.

The once-majestic kingdom of the Nile was not the last region that the Muslims had their eyes on. From Egypt, they moved across North Africa. They planned on securing the Maghreb, a region that encompassed Tunisia, Algeria, and Morocco. However, this was not an easy task. The Muslims had to go through rugged terrains and face the local Berber tribes, which were fiercely independent. Unlike the series of campaigns they took against the Sassanians and the Byzantines, the Muslims spent five decades on military campaigns and diplomacy to bring the region under their control. After securing this region in North Africa, the Muslims began pushing into the Iberian Peninsula. Their success marked the beginning of over seven centuries of Muslim presence in parts of Europe.

The extent of the Islamic expansion by the time of the Umayyad Caliphate.⁴¹

Christian Communities Following the Muslim Conquests

Following these conquests, Christian communities living in the Middle East, North Africa, and the Iberian Peninsula found themselves under new political authorities. Even though the conquest introduced various changes to administration and governance, the Muslims did not immediately erase the existing influence of Christianity in these regions. Instead, these communities adapted, restructured, and, in many cases, maintained continuity under Islamic rule.

It was indeed a challenge for Muslim rulers to govern such vast populations, many of whom did not share their faith. They came up with a system known as dhimma. Since Islam recognized both Christians and Jews as "People of the Book," they were granted protected status. They were given the freedom—up to a certain degree, of course—to practice their religion. They were allowed to maintain their churches and manage their internal affairs, including family law and clerical appointments. However, this tolerance was not given to them without compensation. Under this system, they had to acknowledge the supremacy of the Islamic state and pay a special tax known as the jizya.

Dhimmis (the individuals living under the dhimma system) were often subject to certain legal and social restrictions. They were not allowed to carry weapons, and they could not build new churches unless they were given permission. It was prohibited for them to attempt to convert Muslims to Christianity. Depending on their local leaders, they also had to be extra careful about how openly they practiced their faith.

Nonetheless, many Christian communities were still able to live or even thrive while under Islamic rule. Religious leaders like bishops, priests, and patriarchs were given the chance to retain their roles. In major cities like Damascus, Alexandria, and Jerusalem, churches continued to function as centers of spiritual and communal life.

Large populations of Christians in Syria and Iraq flourished for centuries under these new political authorities. Syriac-speaking Christians played a crucial role in preserving classical knowledge. They were in charge of translating Greek philosophical and medical texts into Arabic, which greatly contributed to the intellectual life of the Islamic Golden Age. Interestingly, the Coptic Orthodox Church in Egypt remained a strong influence among the native population. Even though Arabic gradually replaced Coptic in administration and later in daily life, religious traditions were preserved. Coptic Christians remained the majority in Egypt for at least two centuries; Muslims likely became the majority in Egypt beginning in the 10th century.

Unsurprisingly, peace and tolerance were not always in the air. There were times when non-Muslims faced stricter enforcement of dhimma rules, which typically took place during periods of political unrest or religious tension. One notable episode occurred when the infamous Fatimid Caliph al-Hakim bi-Amr Allah took the reins in the early 11th century. The caliph was known for his erratic policies. He tolerated non-Muslims during the first few years of his reign, but he later imposed harsh restrictions. He even went to the extent of ordering the destruction of the Church of the Holy Sepulchre in 1009 CE. Being a major pilgrimage site for Christians, this decision shocked many and strained diplomatic ties with the Byzantine Empire. The caliph also imposed outrageous regulations in Egypt, where Christians were required to wear distinctive clothing. Many churches faced destruction, and their wealth was confiscated. Throughout his reign, Christians faced pressure to convert. Fortunately, some of these decrees were reversed after his death, allowing Christians to breathe slightly easier.

As for North Africa, its Christian population witnessed a sharp decline over the centuries. Although many communities initially survived for several generations, especially during the early years of conquest, Arabization and Islamization soon took place. This eventually led to the near disappearance of indigenous Christian groups by the 12th century. Factors contributing to this decline include conversion, emigration, and even assimilation. In contrast to the Levant or Egypt, North Africa did not retain a strong Christian institutional presence in the long term.

Christian communities in Spain were referred to as Mozarabs. These were Christians who kept their religion but had already adopted many aspects of the Arabic language and culture in their daily lives. They were also subjected to jizya like other dhimmis. Their churches and religious practices (known as the Mozarabic liturgy) persisted, operating mainly in big cities such as Toledo and Córdoba. However, things changed in the 9th and 10th centuries as tensions between Christians and Muslims occasionally escalated.

Nevertheless, despite many obstacles, many Christian communities survived under Muslim rule for centuries.

Cultural Exchange and Contributions

Centuries after the Muslim conquests, the world saw the emergence of a remarkable era of cultural and intellectual exchange, which unfolded between Christian and Muslim communities. This could be seen especially during the Islamic Golden Age, which spanned from the 8th to the 13th century. These communities often interacted not only in scholarly spheres but also in the realm of art and commerce, eventually contributing to a legacy of shared knowledge that would leave an almost permanent mark across continents.

Many may agree that one of the most notable areas of exchange was in the field of translation. The capital of the Abbasid Caliphate, Baghdad, was home to the House of Wisdom (Hikmat al-Bayt). Christian scholars flocked to this popular center of learning. Here, they were often tasked to translate texts written in Greek, Syriac, and other classical languages into Arabic.

Nestorian Christian scholars, many of whom were fluent in Greek and Syriac, translated works of ancient thinkers like Aristotle, Galen, and Hippocrates. Hunayn ibn Ishaq is considered the chief translator of the 9th century. A Nestorian physician, he became renowned for his precise and systematic translations of medical and philosophical texts. His work made it possible for Arabs to preserve Hellenistic science, which was then integrated into the Islamic intellectual tradition. His translations into Arabic served as primary sources for Latin translations in medieval Europe, which contributed to sparking the Renaissance centuries later.

The exchange was not limited to texts. Many Christian physicians, who were typically well versed in Greek traditions, were given positions in the courts of caliphs and sultans. The Muslims respected their expertise, especially since they were instrumental in shaping Islamic medicine. It was common for hospitals in major cities like Baghdad, Damascus, and Cairo to employ Christian staff members. They usually collaborated with their Muslim peers in the treatment of patients and the advancement of medical practices.

In the world of architecture and art, Christian and Muslim influences blended together. This could be seen especially in al-Andalus. In cities like Córdoba and Toledo, Mozarabic Christians adopted the Arabic script and aesthetic elements, while Islamic architecture occasionally drew upon Roman and Visigothic techniques. This resulted in unique, hybrid forms of architecture. The horseshoe arch is a great example; this particular structure could be seen in both churches and mosques.

An example of the horseshoe arch.⁴⁸

Another notable example that bore this architectural blend was the city of Madinat al-Zahra. Commissioned in the 10th century by Umayyad Caliph Abd al-Rahman III, the city was constructed near Córdoba. Despite being primarily an Islamic palace-city, Madinat al-Zahra featured elements of late antique and Visigothic architecture. Its columns, mosaics, and decorative motifs show influences that can be traced to earlier Roman and Christian traditions.

Episodes of Persecutions

Persecutions against Christians still occurred under Muslim rule, though rarely. Compared to the empire-wide persecutions of Christians conducted under Roman rule, persecutions under Muslim governance were generally more episodic. They were not intended to eradicate Christianity as a whole; rather, they were in response to political instability, ideological reform movements, or suspicions of Christian collaboration with foreign powers. Although not always systematic, we should not dismiss these brutal episodes, as they left a deep impact on Christian populations.

One significant persecution took place in the mid-9th century. It all began when some Christians in Córdoba felt that their traditions and faith were fading away. The Umayyad Emirate of Córdoba allowed Christians to practice their beliefs under certain conditions, but the city had become increasingly Arabized, with Islamic influences taking over many aspects of language and culture. A number of Christians in the city, many of them monks, priests, and devout laypeople, chose to take a stand, hoping they could put a stop to the Arabization.

These people deliberately defied Islamic authorities by making public declarations against both Islam and the Prophet Muhammad. Some were even bold enough to convert from Islam back to Christianity. In Islamic law, both blasphemy and apostasy are considered serious offenses. Blasphemy, especially when directed at the Prophet Muhammad, was treated as an attack on the sanctity of the religion itself. Meanwhile, the act of apostasy, where one abandoned Islam after accepting it, was viewed, at the time, as a betrayal of the faith and the community. (It is worth noting that while Islamic law at the time treated apostasy and blasphemy as capital offenses, modern-day interpretations and enforcement of these laws vary widely across the Muslim world.) Yet, these defiant Christians were not afraid. They did not express themselves in secret. They appeared before judges or stated their declarations in public. Islamic judges, or qadis, applied the standard jurisprudence of the time, which called for capital punishment in such cases if the accused did not recant. A wave of executions was set in motion, which spanned approximately nine years, from 850 to 859 CE.

During this time, a priest and chronicler named Eulogius of Córdoba rose to prominence among the Christians. He was a strong voice for the Christian community, especially those who chose to put a stop to the growing Muslim presence. The priest often visited prisons where arrested Christians were being held. He would remain there for a while, encouraging them to stay firm in their beliefs. In his eyes, what his fellow Christian brothers were doing was heroic and spiritually noble. He offered these prisoners comfort, especially those who were about to face execution. Eulogius also documented the courage of these martyrs in his book, *Memorial of the Saints*. Unfortunately, being a strong voice amidst the community meant the priest was not spared from punishment. He was eventually arrested for helping a Muslim-born convert named Leocritia escape from her family. Refusing to deny his actions or renounce his faith, Eulogius was executed in 859. He was later honored as a saint.

The martyrdom of Eulogius of Córdoba.[48]

This unfortunate period of time also claimed the lives of two women, Flora and Maria. Flora had been born to a Muslim father and a Christian mother. According to Islamic law, if the father was a Muslim, then his children were automatically considered Muslim by birth, regardless of the mother's faith. Therefore, Flora was legally recognized as a Muslim despite being raised as a Christian. When she refused to identify as a Muslim, Flora was accused of apostasy. She was tried and later executed in 851.

Maria was born to two Christian parents. She was not a Muslim under Islamic law. However, when she publicly denounced Islam—sources claim she insulted the Prophet Muhammad—Maria was arrested and put on trial. She was executed in the same year as Flora.

Six years later, another influential priest became a victim of the persecution. Known simply as Roderick, his story began following a domestic dispute between his two brothers—one was a Christian, while the other was a Muslim. Seeing that the dispute was escalating into violence, Roderick intervened and was left seriously injured. Once he had regained consciousness, Roderick discovered that his Muslim brother had taken advantage of him by falsely registering him as a Muslim. In the eyes of Islamic law, Roderick was now a Muslim.

Refusing to change his faith, Roderick continued to live openly as a Christian priest. Things went south when the authorities finally discovered this. He was arrested and charged with apostasy. Although he knew what his fate would be, the priest refused to deny his Christian faith. He was thrown into prison, where he met another Christian convert named Salomon. Unsurprisingly, the two were found guilty of apostasy and subjected to execution in 857. The stories of Flora, Maria, and Roderick were recorded by Eulogius of Córdoba.

Another episode of repression occurred in the eastern provinces of the caliphate during the reign of Abbasid Caliph al-Mutawakkil (r. 847–861 CE). Under the rulers before him, non-Muslims were able to enjoy a degree of freedom. However, when al-Mutawakkil claimed the mantle, he wasted no time in reversing the more lenient policies of his predecessors. Under his rule, Christians and Jews were ordered to wear distinctive clothing so that he could easily segregate them from the Muslim population. They were also no longer allowed to obtain certain positions in public offices. Worst of all, churches were demolished or repurposed, and public displays of Christian symbols were widely curtailed.

The caliph was assassinated in 861 CE, ushering in a period of political instability. The caliphate's central authority was weakened. Because of this, strict policies against non-Muslims were no longer consistently enforced. In some regions, Christians and Jews were able to experience relief as local governors or officials were more lenient.

Similar things happened in North Africa as it entered the 12th century. During this time, the people were governed by the Almohads, a Berber Muslim dynasty originating in the Atlas Mountains. The rulers of this dynasty promoted a stricter and more puritanical form of Islam. Unlike the relatively tolerant Almoravids who preceded them, the Almohads demanded conformity and persecuted those who did not adopt their doctrine. Christian and Jewish communities in Morocco, for instance, were told to embrace Islam and abandon their original beliefs. If they refused to convert, they were given an option to go into exile. If they refused both conversion and exile and still practiced their faith openly, they would have to face the possibility of being executed. Many churches and synagogues were not spared from the Almohads. They were usually destroyed or converted into mosques. These policies undoubtedly caused a significant exodus of Christians and Jews. Others went into hiding or practiced their faith in secret.

Even in times of general stability, local flare-ups of violence and persecution could still occur due to rumors, local disputes, or changes in leadership. There was always a possibility of abrupt changes being made regarding the treatment of Christians, especially when they saw the rise of a new governor or qadi (Islamic judge) who adhered to stricter interpretations of Islamic law. There were also cases where Christians were accused of collaborating with foreign Christian powers, especially during times of war or crusades. This further fueled suspicion and reprisals.

Although these episodes of persecution were real and left a lasting impact, they alone do not capture the full complexity of Christian life under Islamic rule. Across different times and places, many Christian communities experienced periods of stability, coexistence, and even intellectual contribution. Their daily lives were shaped not only by legal restrictions but also by local customs, relationships, and the broader political climate. Like much of history, their experience was not defined by a single narrative but by a spectrum of realities ranging from hardship to resilience.

However, the world would soon witness a shift in the dynamic between Muslim and Christian power. With the onset of the Crusades in 1096 and the gradual advance of Christian kingdoms in the Iberian Peninsula, open conflict became the norm once again.

Chapter 9 – The Crusaders' Blind Spot: Brothers in Name, Strangers in Spirit

A big crowd could be seen making haste to gather outside the cathedral in the town of Clermont (located in what is now central France). It was late November 1095, and they had heard news that Pope Urban II would make an appearance to address a certain matter. Nobles and knights arrived on horseback, monks came on foot, and the townsfolk left their work, all curious to listen to what the pope had prepared. When Pope Urban finally appeared, the air was immediately filled with silence.

"Our Christian brothers in the East have been suffering," the pope might have spoken.

He told the people how, for centuries, the Christians in the East had been pushed aside by Muslim rulers. He explained how their brothers and sisters could no longer worship the Lord freely. He painted a place where holy places were desecrated, burned in flames, or repurposed into Islamic centers. The pope then told the people that if left untreated, the Church of the Holy Sepulchre would soon disappear from the face of the earth. Jerusalem was in foreign hands, and it was high time to reclaim it.

"Go," he urged the public. "Help your fellow Christians. Take back the Holy Land. March under the cross, and know that by doing so, your sins will be forgiven,"

The effect was electric. The air was pierced with shouts coming from thousands of people.

"Deus vult!" they shouted in unison. "God wills!"

Pope Urban II preaching the First Crusade at Clermont."

In the weeks that followed, preparations began. Nobles pledged their armies in the name of Christ. Poor farmers were headstrong in freeing their Christian brothers and left their fields. They gathered what weapons they had and, alongside a few lower-ranking soldiers and knights, marched beyond their walls that spring, claiming to fight under the cross. These inexperienced troops were not officially organized by the Catholic Church. They were simply inspired by the pope's call for a holy expedition. Known as the People's Crusade, their mission ended in disaster. After wreaking havoc in Europe, many were eventually ambushed by the Seljuk Turks and wiped out. The official Crusader armies of the First Crusade, on the other hand, began to march in the summer of 1096.

The pope had inspired many. They raced to free their Christian brothers from Muslim rule. Yet, they were unaware that the Christian world they would encounter was far more diverse than they had imagined—and not all of it would be welcomed. In the eyes of the Crusaders, Christianity wore a Latin face, spoke with a Latin tongue, and worshiped according to Roman rites. The Eastern Christians they encountered did not fit that image. They noticed that their robes were different. Despite honoring the same god, their prayers were sung in unfamiliar words or style. The Copts of Egypt, for example, prayed in the ancient tongue of the pharaohs. The Maronites of Mount Lebanon worshiped in Syriac. There were also those who kept the teachings of Christ alive in Aramaic, the very language Jesus spoke. Despite centuries of shared beliefs, these communities of Eastern Christians were often treated not as kin but as strangers. At best, they were seen as forgotten cousins of the faith. At worst, they were seen as heretics.

Before the Storm

Believe it or not, some of the oldest Christian communities in the world found a foothold in cities like Antioch, Alexandria, Edessa, and the Nineveh Plains, not Rome or Constantinople. These were the places where the early apostles had walked and places where churches had stood for centuries.

These often-overlooked Christian communities—the Maronites, Copts, Syriac Christians, and Assyrians—had gone through multiple episodes of change. They witnessed and survived the fall of the Roman Empire. They were around when the Byzantines rose to prominence, and they also saw the gradual growth of Islamic influence in the 7th century. Despite experiencing cities changing hands and rulers rising and falling, these communities never failed to hold on to their faith.

Even under Islamic rule, they continued to live. Religious tolerance was practiced, although the Christians had to pay a tax. Most of the time, they were allowed to keep their churches, elect their bishops, and maintain their customs. As long as they remained loyal, paid the jizya, and did not provoke the ruling power, these communities were safe. Of course, there were instances where they had to endure hardship and persecution, yet these did not occur as frequently as many may think. Most of the Eastern Christians did what so many ancient communities did best: they adapted, not by surrendering their beliefs and faiths but by learning how to coexist.

The Copts of Egypt continued to pray in Coptic, although Arabic was becoming more commonly used in their daily lives. Their churches featured icons and hymns that dated back to the early Christian Church. They were also led by the Coptic pope in Alexandria, a spiritual figure who held great authority among his people. The Syriac Orthodox Church (sometimes referred to as the Jacobite Church) kept the Aramaic tongue alive, as well as the liturgy of Saint James. Their monasteries in the hills of Tur Abdin and Qartmin became centers of learning. These were the very places where monks copied manuscripts by candlelight and preserved theology, medicine, and philosophy in books bound in leather.

The Monastery of Saint Ananias in Tur Abdin (three kilometers southeast of Mardin, Turkey)."

Farther east, the Assyrian Church of the East—often labeled Nestorian by outsiders—had carved out its own identity. Despite being cut off from both Rome and Constantinople, it had spread far beyond its homeland, sending missionaries across Persia, Central Asia, and even into China. Their bishops governed flocks across a vast land, speaking languages as varied as their terrain. The Maronites, however, lived in relative isolation amidst the mountains of Lebanon. They worshiped in Syriac and held strong to their monastic traditions. Although their theological alignment with Rome would later evolve, at this time, they were part of the wider Eastern Christian mosaic.

These Eastern Christians were not confined to just their churches and monasteries. In major cities like Damascus, Baghdad, and Cairo, Christians served as doctors, translators, merchants, and scribes. They were respected in some courts and resented in others. There were many instances where Christians held official posts in Islamic courts. These positions reflected a degree of trust and coexistence. However, it might have stirred unease among the Crusaders, who were unfamiliar with such arrangements. For the Latin newcomers, this cooperation could be misunderstood as a compromise or, worse, allegiance.

It is safe to assume that despite being governed by rulers of different faiths, the Eastern Christians were still part of the Christian world. What they did not expect was to be seen as strangers by those who arrived in the name of the same faith. When news of the Crusades slowly reached them, many were hopeful. Perhaps these Western Christians were coming to reclaim Jerusalem in the name of Christ and lend a hand to support their Eastern brothers, strengthening the church on both sides of the world. Although the Crusaders did restore Christian rule over parts of this region, some communities ended up being overlooked.

The Arrival of the Crusaders

The first major wave of Crusaders crossed into the Levant sometime in the autumn of 1097. After enduring months of marching across Europe and Anatolia, they finally arrived at the great cities of the eastern Mediterranean. Some of these places, including Antioch, Edessa, and Jerusalem, were familiar to them; they had heard of their names through scripture and legend. However, they only knew the names of these places, not their traditions and customs. The world they entered was definitely not what they expected.

They knew that the people here shared the same faith as they did. But why did they pray in languages unfamiliar to the Latin ear? Even their saints had names that they rarely heard of in the West. The Eastern Christians honored Saint Ephrem the Syrian, Saint Maron, Saint Shenouda, and Saint Isaac of Nineveh. The West was more familiar with names like Saint Benedict, Saint Augustine, and Saint Martin of Tours.

The Crusaders also noticed the distinct appearance of their crosses. It was common for the cross in Latin churches to appear rather plain and symmetrical. However, in the East, one might see Coptic crosses with flared ends, Byzantine crosses with additional horizontal bars, or Nestorian crosses enclosed within circles. These variations undoubtedly contributed to the Crusaders' sense of unease.

An early form of a Coptic cross.[46]

The Crusaders reached the gates of Antioch, one of Christianity's most ancient and revered cities, in October 1097. They besieged the city, but the defenders—Seljuk Turks under the command of Yaghi-Siyan— refused to give up easily. They held firm behind the massive stone walls. When winter came, the Crusaders were troubled with multiple obstacles. Food was scarce, and disease spread through their camps. Their morale also began to shake. Nevertheless, the Crusaders were not planning on retreating. The siege went on for eight grueling months.

The city was eventually breached by June 1098 when the Crusaders combined their persistence with a secret arrangement with an Armenian guard inside the city. They poured into Antioch, bringing down anyone who stood in their way. However, their victory was short-lived. A few days later, the tables were turned; the Crusaders found themselves besieged in the very city they had breached by a Muslim army led by Kerbogha of Mosul. The Crusaders held out, rallying around what they believed to be the Holy Lance, and eventually forced Kerbogha to retreat.

With Antioch finally in their grasp, the Crusaders worked to take control of not only its streets and towers but also its religious authority. They were not planning on maintaining continuity with the established Greek Orthodox Church. The Crusaders moved against Patriarch John VII the Oxite, who had been appointed by the Byzantine emperor himself. Despite being a respected figure among local Christians, John was unable to do anything when he was exiled. The former patriarch fled to Constantinople, where he lived out the rest of his years. In his place, the Crusaders installed a Latin patriarch, Bernard of Valence, a Norman cleric hailing from France who had been accompanying the Crusader forces. This immediate shift from Eastern Orthodox to Latin Church authority in Antioch marked a major rupture between Western and Eastern Christianity. While the Crusaders saw their action as a necessary correction, some of the local Eastern Christians viewed it as an erasure of their heritage.

The Crusaders taking over Jerusalem."

The Crusaders reached Jerusalem the following year in early June 1099. At the time, the city was under the control of the Fatimid

Caliphate. Despite being crippled with a lack of resources (food, water, and siege equipment), the Crusaders prevailed. They constructed siege towers and ladders, which they used to besiege the city for a month. The final assault was launched in July of the same year, where they succeeded in breaching and entering the city. The scene turned bloody almost immediately. A massacre began, with the Crusaders killing many of the city's inhabitants. In the confusion and violence, not only were Muslims and Jews massacred, but the Crusaders were also said to have misunderstood the identities of the Eastern Christians. They also fell victim to the Crusaders' swords.

Interestingly, the Greek Orthodox Patriarch Symeon had already been exiled from Jerusalem by the Fatimids before the siege even began. The Crusaders used the opportunity to install a Latin patriarch to oversee the Church of the Holy Sepulchre, along with other crucial Christian sites. The Church of the Holy Sepulchre was seen as the most important goal of their conquest. To them, placing it firmly under Latin ecclesiastical authority ensured religious cohesion and strengthened the legitimacy of their campaign.

Although Eastern clergy were allowed to remain, with a Latin patriarch installed, their roles became more limited. Eastern Christians were not prohibited from worshiping there, but they had to agree to certain restrictions. They were only allowed to perform their religious services at certain hours. More often than not, priority was given to Latin clergy, so the Eastern Christians had to wait until Latin ceremonies were finished before they could use the space. There were also instances where they were relegated to side chapels.

The reception the Crusaders received from Eastern Christians was mixed. They were undoubtedly welcomed by Christian communities that had been suffering under recent Muslim rulers or military campaigns. But they were also met with polite distance or even silent alarm. Many local Christians hoped the Crusaders would be allies, protectors even, but the relationship somehow gradually became one-sided.

Eastern Christian communities in the Levant saw the arrival of more Latin rulers in the years following the First Crusade. The Copts, Syriac Orthodox, Armenians, Melkites, and others had practiced their faith for centuries under different rulers. They thrived under both the Byzantine Empire and the Islamic caliphates. The arrival of the Crusaders introduced a different kind of relationship. Over time, their traditions were no longer central. Liturgies in Syriac, Coptic, or Armenian were less visible. Decisions about church governance were made without their input at times. In some cases, they were expected to defer to clerics newly arrived from Europe who were unfamiliar with the local scene and customs.

Many Crusaders were unfamiliar with Eastern languages and theology, so they struggled to distinguish between the various Christian sects. Terms like Miaphysitism or Nestorian, which carried specific theological meanings in the East, were often misunderstood or even oversimplified in the West. This eventually led to occasional suspicion, especially of local Christians who were found to have longstanding relationships with Muslim neighbors. This could be seen when the Crusaders took the city of Edessa. At first, the Crusaders enjoyed support from some local Christian groups, including the Armenians and Syriac Orthodox. Things began to change when tensions increased between Crusader leaders and neighboring Muslim leaders. The Crusaders began to look at the local Christian communities differently. They wondered if they were sympathetic to the Muslims, especially since they had coexisted with the Muslims for centuries.

In 1144, Edessa was recaptured by the Muslims, who were under the command of Zengi. This was considered a major loss for the Crusaders, especially since Edessa was the first Crusader State to have been established. Interestingly, there is little evidence of widespread panic or mass flight when Zengi claimed the city. Many local Christians chose to remain in Edessa. They preferred the stability under familiar Muslim rule compared to the uncertainties that came with the relatively new Latin Crusader administration.

Michael the Syrian, the 12th-century patriarch of the Syriac Orthodox Church, recounted not only political events but also the lived experiences of his community in his *Chronicle*. His writings were not an open condemnation of the Crusaders but merely a reflection of his concern. He wrote about times when Eastern Christians were viewed with mistrust or overlooked entirely, despite having prayed to the same Lord. Through his writings, the patriarch expressed his disappointment, not in the Crusaders' intentions but in their limited understanding of the traditions and histories already present in the East.

Of course, Michael never confronted the Latin Church. Instead, he focused on preservation. He encouraged the teaching of Syriac, the copying of manuscripts, and the quiet continuation of ancient rites. His efforts helped ensure that the identity of the Syriac Church would endure, even as the balance of power shifted around it.

Diplomacy has always been the key to navigating complex situations. In places like Antioch, Edessa, and Tripoli, Eastern Christian clergy and nobles sought ways to engage with both Latin and Muslim authorities. Prince Toros I and later Prince Ruben of Cilician Armenia, for instance, were known to have cooperated with the Crusaders. In exchange for political recognition and military alliances, they agreed to provide aid and supplies to the Crusaders. Indeed, these relationships were not always easy, but by doing this, the Armenian Christians were given a chance to assert their autonomy.

Another great example comes from the Maronite Christians on Mount Lebanon. Despite having developed a strong monastic tradition and a distinct liturgical identity that was deeply rooted in Syriac Christianity, the Maronites chose to enter into full communion with the Roman Catholic Church. This was not a forced submission. Instead, it was a decision shaped by both religious affinity and political foresight. The Maronites were able to establish closer ties with the Latin Church, and they were also allowed to position themselves as valuable allies of the Crusaders. In exchange, they were given security, papal recognition, and autonomy. This particular relationship would endure long after the Crusaders departed.

Elsewhere, particularly in areas where governance changed hands frequently, communities chose neutrality. The Assyrians and Syriac Christians in the Nineveh Plains and parts of Upper Mesopotamia often choose to avoid entanglement in military campaigns. Instead, they focused more on preserving their monasteries, schools, and local traditions. They also maintained relations with Muslim leaders who were familiar with their presence and, when possible, kept their distance from Crusader politics. The Coptic Orthodox Church continued to exist in Fatimid Egypt. While they were aware of the Crusades—especially when Jerusalem and parts of the Levant changed hands—their survival depended more on maintaining a working relationship with the ruling caliphate. The Copts, like their Syriac counterparts, understood that political favor could shift quickly.

It is important to note that not all of their encounters with the Crusaders were tense or distant. There were times when Eastern

Christians served as interpreters, mediators, and even advisors to Latin leaders. The Crusaders treasured the people's knowledge of local geography, customs, and diplomacy, especially when they were in an unfamiliar terrain. Although these roles were sometimes limited, they allowed certain individuals and communities the opportunity to preserve their influence and safeguard their people.

Of course, with strategies came risks. Aligning too closely with either side had consequences, especially when the tides of power changed. Local Christians in Aleppo or Damascus, for instance, had to tread carefully when tensions arose over Crusader raids. Even the slightest hint of collaboration could result in harsh punishment or increased restrictions. Likewise, those who were seen as reluctant to support the Crusaders might find themselves marginalized within the newly formed Latin principalities.

Despite these challenges, many communities chose to focus inward, strengthening their cultural and spiritual roots. Monasteries became more than places of worship. They became centers of literacy, social cohesion, and historical memory. Monks copied ancient texts, trained young clergy, and passed on local histories in languages like Syriac, Coptic, and Armenian. Through this quiet resilience, they ensured that their identities would not be erased by the politics of war.

However, it is safe to say that the landscape of faith in the Middle East during the Crusades was far more complex than a simple Christian-Muslim divide. Within the Christian world itself, there were layers of language, theology, and tradition, and these layers did not always align. There were times when they clashed. Regardless, it was within this very mosaic of belief that the Eastern Christian communities found ways to endure. They did so not by seeking dominance but by preserving what was there with patience and faith.

Conclusion

If Christian history were a grand cathedral, the stories that we have explored in this book would not rest on the well-polished altar or even beneath the central dome. Instead, these stories would be found along the outer cloisters and hidden chapels. These quieter spaces—the lesser-known stories, the nearly forgotten figures, the gospels that never made it into the Bible—are important. They do not challenge the foundation of the cathedral but instead enrich its design. These stories add texture, depth, and unexpected beauty. They remind us that Christian history has always been deeper and more varied than any single telling can fully capture.

We have stepped outside the familiar bounds of Christian history. We have looked through the lens of the Apostles who traveled east instead of west. We were introduced to Christian communities that sang hymns in Syriac, Coptic, and Gaelic rather than Latin or Greek. We have traveled to the unknown desert, listening to the voices of the Desert Fathers whose resilience was undeniable, and heard stories of women who shaped faith not by titles but by example. We have also taken a glimpse into the gospels labeled "apocryphal," not to undermine the canon but to understand what those texts meant to the communities that treasured them. Perhaps most importantly, we have seen beyond the lens of power and victory by stepping into the shoes of communities in the East that were often overlooked and misunderstood for their distinct traditions.

It is clear that Christianity has never been one single tradition moving in a straight line. It has always been a movement of many threads. Even from the beginning, it has taken many forms, shaped throughout the centuries by different cultures, conflicts, and relationships.

Of course, this book is not the end of the story but rather an invitation for those curious enough to keep learning, to find what else has been left in the shadows. Perhaps some of these stories will lead to further study. Perhaps others will simply settle in your heart as quiet echoes, reminders that the past is never truly the past and that what was hidden may yet speak again.

Here's another book by Matt Clayton that you might like

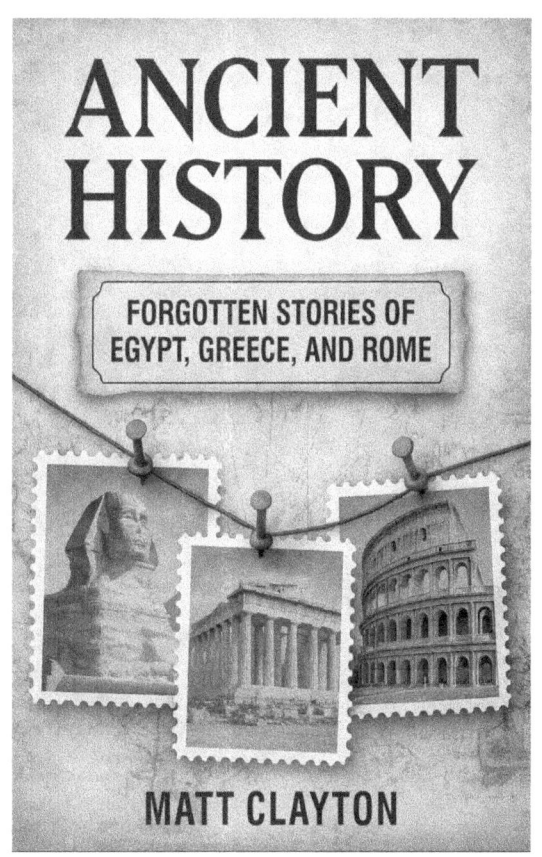

Free Bonus from Captivating History (Available for a Limited time)

Hi History Lovers!

Now you have a chance to join our exclusive history list so you can get your first history ebook for free as well as discounts and a potential to get more history books for free!

Simply visit the link below to join.

Or, Scan the QR code!

captivatinghistory.com/ebook

Also, make sure to follow us on Facebook, X, and YouTube by searching for Captivating History.

Bibliography

Allison, Matthew, and Unknown Artist. "Christianity in Japan." *World History Encyclopedia*, Aug. 2024, www.worldhistory.org/article/2503/christianity-in-japan.

Carr, Simonetta. "Alopen and the Missionary Monks of the Church of the East." *Place for Truth*, 23 Nov. 2021, www.placefortruth.org/blog/alopen-and-the-missionary-monks-of-the-church-of-the-east.

Cartwright, Mark, and G. Dallorto. "Saint Gregory the Illuminator." *World History Encyclopedia*, Mar. 2025, www.worldhistory.org/Saint_Gregory_the_Illuminator.

"The Catholic Defender: Saint David of Wales." *Deeper Truth*, www.deepertruthcatholics.com/single-post/the-catholic-defender-saint-david-of-wales. Accessed 22 Mar. 2025.

Cohick, Lynn H. "Priscilla and Aquila." *Bible Odyssey*.

"Cross of St. Nino." *Georgia.to*, georgia.to/cross-of-saint-nino. Accessed 15 Mar. 2025.

"Cul Dreimhne – The Battle of the Book." *Dispatches From the Former New World*, 20 Sept. 2017, https://dispatchesfromtheformernewworld.com/2017/09/20/cul-dreimhne-the-battle-of-the-book/

Devil_U_Dont_Know. "The Myth of St. Thomas." *Medium*, 17 Feb. 2020, medium.com/@TheSensible_1/the-myth-of-st-thomas-7ef88ecb9e13.

"Did you know that St. Benedict was nearly poisoned twice?" *The Catholic Company*, https://www.catholiccompany.com/blogs/get-fed/did-you-know-that-st-benedict-was-nearly-poisoned-twice#:~:text=Some%2520of%2520the%2520monks%2520grew,cup%E2%80%94and%2520it%2520instantly%2520shattered . Accessed 14 Mar. 2025.

Graves, Dan. "Frumentius Begged a Bishop for Ethiopia—and He Was It." *Christian History Institute*, https://christianhistoryinstitute.org/dailystory/permalink/frumentius-begged-a-bishop-for-ethiopia-and-he-was-it . Accessed 22 Mar. 2025.

"How The Synod Of Whitby Settled The Date Of Easter." *English Heritage*, www.english-heritage.org.uk/visit/places/whitby-abbey/history-and-stories/easter-and-the-synod-of-whitby. Accessed 22 Mar. 2025.

Jenkins, Andrew. "From Slave to Missionary: Meet St. Patrick." *Core Christianity*, 13 Mar. 2023, https://corechristianity.com/resources/articles/from-slave-to-missionary-meet-st-patrick .

Johnson, Alex. "Olga of Kiev: The One Saint You Don't Want to Mess With." *Museum Hack*, 20 Nov. 2022, https://museumhack.com/olga-of-kiev.

Johnson, Ben. "St Andrew, Patron Saint of Scotland." *Historic UK*, www.historic-uk.com/HistoryUK/HistoryofScotland/St-Andrew-Patron-Saint-of-Scotland. Accessed 20 Mar. 2025.

LotusBuddhas. "Who Were the Twelve Apostles? Their Lives and Legacies." *LotusBuddhas*, 4 July 2024, https://lotusbuddhas.com/who-were-the-twelve-apostles.html.

Marina, Marko. "The Gospel Of Thomas: Summary And Why It's Not In The Bible." *Bart Ehrman*, 10 Oct. 2023, www.bartehrman.com/gospel-of-thomas.

"The Martyrdom of St. Andrew." *The Holy Catholic Religion*, 30 Nov. 2016, https://holycatholicreligion.blogspot.com/2016/11/the-martyrdom-of-st-andrew.html

"Matteo Ricci, SJ (1552–1610)." *IgnatianSpirituality.com*, www.ignatianspirituality.com/ignatian-voices/16th-and-17th-century-ignatian-voices/matteo-ricci-sj. Accessed 10 Mar. 2025.

Minati Moraes, Jessica de Costa. "Helena of Constantinople." *World History*, 21 Apr. 2022, www.worldhistory.org/Helena_of_Constantinople.

Morgan, David. "A Tale of the Unexpected - Early Chinese Bible Translation." *SIL in Eurasia*, https://eurasia.sil.org/culture-and-society/history_and_religion/a_history_of_the_eastern_church/a_tale_of_the_unexpected . Accessed 10 Mar. 2025.

Niles, Randall. "The Story of Frumentius." *Drive Thru History*, 23 Apr. 2021, https://drivethruhistory.com/the-story-of-frumentius/?srsltid=AfmBOoo-0RpYgJYfaeuT80XFbsr1UiZ3Q7gAFTMkbhcHCUixkXzjpvOY

Rausch, Franklin, and Haeseong Park. "Christianity in Korea." *Association for Asian Studies*, www.asianstudies.org/publications/eaa/archives/christianity-in-korea. Accessed 10 Mar. 2025.

"Saint Augustine Of Hippo." *The Augustinians*, https://augustinian.org/spirituality/saint-augustine-of-hippo/. Accessed 19 Mar. 2025.

"Saint Hedwig." *My Catholic Life*, https://mycatholic.life/saints/saints-of-the-liturgical-year/october-17-st-hedwige/. Accessed 18 Mar. 2025.

Smith, Jeb. "Revisiting the Crusades: Defense, Faith, and Survival." *Medieval History*, 25 Aug. 2024, https://historymedieval.com/revisiting-the-crusades-defense-faith-and-survival/.

"Venerable and God-bearing Father Anthony the Great." *Orthodox Church in America*, www.oca.org/saints/lives/2025/01/17/100216-venerable-and-god-bearing-father-anthony-the-great. Accessed 24 Mar. 2025.

"Venerable Pachomius the Great, Founder of Coenobitic Monasticism." *Orthodox Church in America*, www.oca.org/saints/lives/2015/05/15/101384-venerable-pachomius-the-great-founder-of-coenobitic-monasticism. Accessed 24 Mar. 2025.

Wallace, J. Warner. "Why Shouldn't We Trust The Non-Canonical Gospels Attributed To Bartholomew?" *Cold Case Christianity*, 4 Mar. 2016, https://coldcasechristianity.com/writings/why-shouldnt-we-trust-the-non-canonical-gospels-attributed-to-bartholomew/.

Wallace, J. Warner. "Why Shouldn't We Trust The Non-Canonical Gospels Attributed To Peter?" *Cold Case Christianity*, 23 Mar. 2028, https://coldcasechristianity.com/writings/why-shouldnt-we-trust-the-non-canonical-gospels-attributed-to-peter/.

"Who is St. Anthony the Great?" *St. Anthony the Great Orthodox Church*, https://stanthonyorthodoxchurch.com/who-is-st-anthony-the-great/. Accessed 7 Mar. 2025.

Who was Saint Catherine? https://mused.com/stories/40/who-was-saint-catherine/. Accessed 18 Mar. 2025.

Image Sources

1 https://commons.wikimedia.org/wiki/File:Milos,_Bishop_of_Persia,_and_ his_two_disciples_Euoures_the_Presbyter_and_Seboes_the_Deacon.jpg

2 G.dallorto, CC BY 2.5 <https://creativecommons.org/licenses/by/2.5>, via Wikimedia Commons: https://commons.wikimedia.org/wiki/File:Gregory_the_ Illuminator_mosaic_on_Pammakaristos_Church_in_Constantinople.jpg

3 Diego Delso, CC BY-SA 4.0 <https://creativecommons.org/licenses/by-sa/4.0>, via Wikimedia Commons: https://commons.wikimedia.org/wiki/File: Monasterio_Khor_Virap,_Armenia,_2016-10-01,_DD_19.jpg

4 https://commons.wikimedia.org/wiki/File:St_Nino_icon_at_Svetitskhoveli,_ Georgia.JPG

5 https://commons.wikimedia.org/wiki/File:St_Frumentius.jpg

6 Sailko, CC BY 3.0 <https://creativecommons.org/licenses/by/3.0>, via Wikimedia Commons: https://commons.wikimedia.org/wiki/File:Aksum,_chiesa_nuova_di _santa_maria_di_zion,_costruita_da_haile_selassie_negli_anni_%2760,_esterno_00, 0.jpg

7 https://commons.wikimedia.org/wiki/File:Tissot_Moses_and_Joshua_in_the _Tabernacle.jpg

8 https://commons.wikimedia.org/wiki/File:Baptism_- _Ethiopian_Biblical_Manuscript_U.Oregon_Museum_Shelf_Mark_10-844_b.jpg

9 https://commons.wikimedia.org/wiki/File:Demotte_Shahname_002.jpg

10 https://commons.wikimedia.org/wiki/File:Ghirlandaio,_Domenico_- _Calling_of_the_Apostles_-_1481.jpg

11 https://commons.wikimedia.org/wiki/File:Synaxis_of_the_Twelve_ Apostles_by_Constantinople_master_(early_14th_c.,_Pushkin_museum).jpg

12 https://commons.wikimedia.org/wiki/File:Rubens_apostel_andreas_grt.jpg

13 https://commons.wikimedia.org/wiki/File:Andrew_(Menologion_of_Basil_II).jpg

14 Richard Mortel, CC BY 2.0 <https://creativecommons.org/licenses/by/2.0>, via Wikimedia Commons: https://commons.wikimedia.org/wiki/File:Thomas_the_Apostle._Detail_of_the_mosaic_in_the_Basilica_of_San_Vitale._Ravena,_Italy.jpg

15 99v, CC BY-SA 4.0 <https://creativecommons.org/licenses/by-sa/4.0>, via Wikimedia Commons: https://commons.wikimedia.org/wiki/File:Postal_stamp_of_St_Thomas.jpg

16 Richard Mortel, CC BY 2.0 <https://creativecommons.org/licenses/by/2.0>, via Wikimedia Commons: https://commons.wikimedia.org/wiki/File:Bartholomew_the_Apostle._Detail_of_the_mosaic_in_the_Basilica_of_San_Vitale._Ravena,_Italy.jpg

17 https://commons.wikimedia.org/wiki/File:Saint_James_the_Less_(Menologion_of_Basil_II).jpg

18 https://commons.wikimedia.org/wiki/File:Christ_in_the_Wilderness_-_Ivan_Kramskoy_-_Google_Cultural_Institute.jpg

19 https://commons.wikimedia.org/wiki/File:Saint_Anthony_(Damaskinos).png

20 https://commons.wikimedia.org/wiki/File:Michelangelo_Buonarroti_-_The_Torment_of_Saint_Anthony_-_Google_Art_Project.jpg

21 https://commons.wikimedia.org/wiki/File:Memling,_Trittico_di_Benedetto_Portinari,_San_Benedetto.jpg

22 https://commons.wikimedia.org/wiki/File:Saint_Augustine_and_Saint_Monica.jpg

23 https://commons.wikimedia.org/wiki/File:Alexander_Ivanov_-_Christ%27s_Appearance_to_Mary_Magdalene_after_the_Resurrection_-_Google_Art_Project.jpg

24 Brosen, CC BY-SA 3.0 <http://creativecommons.org/licenses/by-sa/3.0/>, via Wikimedia Commons: https://commons.wikimedia.org/wiki/File:Brosen_icon_constantine_helena.jpg

25 https://commons.wikimedia.org/wiki/File:Agnolo_Gaddi_True_Cross_Detail_1380.jpg)

26 https://commons.wikimedia.org/wiki/File:Carlo_Crivelli_014.jpg

27 Museum Plantin-Moretus, CC0, via Wikimedia Commons: https://commons.wikimedia.org/wiki/File:Sint-Paulus_bij_de_heiligen_Aquila_en_Priscilla,_onbekend,_schilderij,_Museum_Plantin-Moretus_(Antwerpen)_-_MPM_V_IV_118.jpg

28 https://commons.wikimedia.org/wiki/File:St_Olga_by_Nesterov_in_1892_(cropped).jpg

29 https://commons.wikimedia.org/wiki/File:A09_Mshenie_Olgi.jpg

30 Reinhardhauke, CC BY-SA 3.0 <https://creativecommons.org/licenses/by-sa/3.0>, via Wikimedia Commons: https://commons.wikimedia.org/wiki/File: Landkern_St._Servatius_10418.JPG

31 https://commons.wikimedia.org/wiki/File:Silk_route.jpg

32 InfernoXV, CC BY-SA 3.0 <http://creativecommons.org/licenses/by-sa/3.0/>, via Wikimedia Commons: https://commons.wikimedia.org/wiki/File:Nantang_NW.jpg

33 Houjyou-Minori, CC0, via Wikimedia Commons: https://commons.wikimedia.org/wiki/File:Oura_Cathedral_20180623.jpg

34 Asacyan, CC BY-SA 4.0 <https://creativecommons.org/licenses/by-sa/4.0>, via Wikimedia Commons: https://commons.wikimedia.org/wiki/File: Myeongdong_Cathedral_01_(cropped).jpg

35 Kang Byeong Kee This photo was taken with Nikon D80, CC BY 3.0 <https://creativecommons.org/licenses/by/3.0>, via Wikimedia Commons: https://commons.wikimedia.org/wiki/File:MyungsungChurch.jpg

36 Albert Bridge / Slemish (8). This file is licensed under the Creative Commons Attribution-Share Alike 2.0 Generic license, https://creativecommons.org/licenses/by-sa/2.0/deed.en: https://commons.wikimedia.org/wiki/File:Slemish_(8)_-_geograph.org.uk_-_834986.jpg

37 Andreas F. Borchert, CC BY-SA 3.0 DE <https://creativecommons.org/licenses/by-sa/3.0/de/deed.en>, via Wikimedia Commons: https://commons.wikimedia.org/wiki/File:Carlow_Cathedral_St_Patrick_Preaching_to_the_Kings_2009_09_03.jpg

38 William Hole, CC BY-SA 3.0 <https://creativecommons.org/licenses/by-sa/3.0>, via Wikimedia Commons: https://commons.wikimedia.org/wiki/File: Saint_Columba_converting_the_Picts.jpg

39 Thruxton, CC BY 3.0 <https://creativecommons.org/licenses/by/3.0>, via Wikimedia Commons: https://commons.wikimedia.org/wiki/File: St_Non%27s_Chapel.JPG

40 https://en.wikipedia.org/wiki/File:Rodrigo_and_Tariq.jpg

41 Constantine Plakidas, CC BY-SA 4.0 <https://creativecommons.org/licenses/by-sa/4.0>, via Wikimedia Commons: https://commons.wikimedia.org/wiki/File:Caliphate_740-en.svg

42 José Antonio Gil Martínez from Vigo, Spain, CC BY 2.0 <https://creativecommons.org/licenses/by/2.0>, via Wikimedia Commons: https://commons.wikimedia.org/wiki/File:Iglesia_de_San_Miguel_de_Escalada_(50 24992819).jpg

43 https://commons.wikimedia.org/wiki/File:EulogioCordovamart.JPG

44 https://commons.wikimedia.org/wiki/File:B_Urban_II2.jpg

45 https://commons.wikimedia.org/wiki/File:Deyrulzaferan.jpg

46 https://commons.wikimedia.org/wiki/File:Codex_Glazier_2.JPG

47 https://commons.wikimedia.org/wiki/File:Taking_of_Jerusalem_by_the_
Crusaders,_15th_July_1099.jpg